HUGH RIPPON

Discovering
English Folk Dance

D0528705

SHIRE PUBLICATIONS LTD

06205466 PPR

Typeset in Plantin by Shire Publications, and printed in Great Britain by CIT Printing Services, Press Buildings, Merlins Bridge, Haverfordwest, Dyfed SA61 1XF.

British Library Cataloguing in Publication Data: Rippon, Hugh. Discovering English Folk Dance. – 3 Rev. ed. – (Discovering Series; No. 206). I. Title. II. Series. 793.31942. ISBN 0-7478-0225-4.

ACKNOWLEDGEMENTS

For this revision the author is particularly grateful to the following for their help: Roy Dommett, Mike Douglass, Brian Pearce, Derek Schofield, Sally Wearing, Charles Arnold, Malcolm Taylor, Theresa Buckland, Trevor Stone, Peter Mayes, Kieth Thompson and Keith Chandler.
Photographs are acknowledged as follows: Cadbury Lamb, pages 2, 6, 9, 13, 41, 45 (upper), 49, 51, 86 and 91; Brian Shuel, pages 8, 23, 24, 28, 30, 38, 53, 54 and 76; Derek Schofield, pages 18, 22 (both), 25, 26, 27, 29, 31, 32, 33, 42 (both), 45 (lower), 46 (both), 47, 48, 63, 67, 83, and cover picture; F. Forster, page 35; and John Rapson, page 36.

Aldbury Morris Men celebrate May morning, 1993, in their Hertfordshire village, dancing by the pond.

Contents

Cover photograph: *The Winster Morris Men, Derbyshire.*

The country maypole from a mid nineteenth-century engraving. Although somewhat idealistic, it does nevertheless show a traditional English maypole outside a tavern. The pole is hung with wreaths.

Foreword

'Well, we didn't know the English had so many dances of their own!' How many times have we heard that said? The fact is that England, being a very mixed nation, is particularly rich in folk dances and folk music, richer than most people appreciate. Moreover, these days the music, songs and dances are to be found performed not only in their original rural settings but also increasingly in large towns and cities where they are the leisure pursuit of a growing number of people of all ages. Thus on most Saturdays in most areas of England it will not be difficult to find a public folk dance being held on modern lines with the traditional folk dances as the main repertoire.

Every summer, too, there are many outdoor festivals or shows of traditional English dance and music organised by the various folk-dance clubs up and down the country. At these you will see many of the traditional English folk dances being performed by men and women, together with special displays of sword and morris dancing either by one of the new revival teams or by one of the older surviving traditional teams.

One of the interesting features of the folk-dance scene in England is the existence of the old and the new alongside each other. In 1911 Cecil Sharp founded the English Folk Dance Society 'to preserve and promote the practice of English folk dances in their true traditional form'. Its aim was to set up new activities where people would learn the traditional dances, songs and music which were in danger of dying out. For example, the ritual sword- and morris-dance teams of men had dwindled from nearly 250 to a few dozen by 1911. In time, however, there were many new teams of younger men anxious to learn from the older teams.

Many widely differing versions of the English ritual morris and sword dances have survived. The most astonishing version probably comes from Bacup in Lancashire, where the dancers appear in blackened faces with garlands or wooden discs called 'nuts' which are clapped in time to the music. Or there is the 'Obby Oss' ceremony in Padstow, Cornwall, where the dancing, twirling hobby-horse appears dressed up like an African medicine-man. There are the horn dancers in Abbots Bromley, Staffordshire, there is the midwinter sword dance ceremony at Grenoside, South Yorkshire, where the captain is symbolically decapitated, and there are the morris dancers dressed in white, who dance at Whitsuntide in Bampton and Headington, Oxfordshire.

All these, and the new activities which have found their inspiration in the old, will be described. It will be shown where to find them and when, and their meaning will also be indicated where possible. Generally speaking, there are two sorts of folk dancing in England: the ritual-ceremonial, which is ceremonial dancing performed by special teams of dancers for a ritual purpose; and social dancing, which is dancing for social occasions for both men, women and children. This two-way division is reflected in the arrangement of the chapters. The revival will also be described, for although folk dance and song nearly died out in England eventually the traditional material came to be much sought after by younger generations looking for a form of expression that is sociable, pleasurable and informal.

Harberton Morris is a family team from Devon. Note the strawberries on the baldricks, because the team's first show was at a strawberry fair.

1
Ritual ceremonial dances in England

There are in England three major forms of the ritual ceremonial dance. The first, and probably the most familiar, is the **Cotswold morris dance** which is found performed by over four hundred teams of dancers all over England. They are distinguished by the presence of six performers dressed mostly in white with coloured sashes or ribbons, hats of various designs decorated with 'spring' flowers and ribbons, and bells and ribbons on their legs. They dance with white handkerchiefs or sticks and are often accompanied by a 'fool' dressed garishly, sometimes as a simple shepherd, sometimes as a circus clown, sometimes even as a 'man-woman'. Often the fool has odd-coloured socks, a painted face, and a bladder and cow's tail attached to a stick. Sometimes there is also a cakebearer who carries a 'good-luck' cake impaled on a sword. The teams used to perform mostly at Whitsuntide but now are to be seen at all times of the year. Originally the dances were performed as part of a procession and most teams still have 'processional on' and 'processional off' dances in their repertoire as vestiges of the old processions. Most of the dances, however, are performed as 'set' dances on one spot with two lines of three men each. Central to each dance is some theme like challenging or fighting, hand clapping, stick clashing, stamping or leaping. At one stage in their evolution the dances must have emulated the fashion in social country dancing and absorbed some of the figures out of the country dances like 'crossing over', 'side by side', or 'back to back'.

Another familiar form of morris dance, but one which operates on a bigger scale and seems to be ideal for larger audiences, is the **processional morris dance**. This is found mostly in north-western England, especially in Lancashire and on the Cheshire Plain, where the dancers used to be an integral part of the annual rushcart procession to church at the end of summer. The number of dancers is indeterminate but is usually at least eight men. They process in two lines, twirling brightly coloured slings or ribboned sticks. From time to time they stop and perform the various figures of a set dance before moving on. Modern teams, however, sometimes concentrate on performing the set dances only because of the

Monkseaton Morris Men, near Newcastle upon Tyne, display the lock in a rapper sword dance, carefully scrutinised by the Betsy, whom some will recognise as the late Alan Brown, who contributed so much to the modern revival movement.

difficulty of processing through crowded modern streets. They used to be accompanied by a black-faced 'man-woman' with a broom, but this figure is rarely seen now. The dancers wear heavily beflowered hats, white shirts, a profusion of ribbons, sashes and beads, breeches and iron-soled clogs. Their music consists of a concertina or accordion band with a bass drum or, in many instances, a fully blown brass band.

The second form of the ritual ceremonial dance in England is the **linked sword dance** originally to be found performed by traditional teams in the north-east (Northumberland, Durham and Yorkshire), but now to be seen everywhere as performed by modern teams of dancers. A team usually consists of five, six or eight men linked together by metal or wooden 'swords' with handles. They perform various circling or intertwining figures, often without breaking the circle, and usually finish with swords locked together in a 'knot' or 'rose'. This is held up for display by the leader of the team. In the rapper version of the sword dance there are five men only and the swords, called 'rappers', are flexible with two handles. Every now and then between the figures the dancers break into a fast tap stepping and on some occasions even a somersault by one of the dancers. In both sorts of dance accompanying characters consist of a male or 'female' or a Tommy and a Betsy. Sometimes the dance is still performed in company with a mummers' play. The traditional season for appearance was Christmas and after.

The third form of ritual ceremonial dance is the **hobby-horse dance** now found in the West Country in four places only. The central figure of the dance is the hobby or wooden horse, which is in fact a man covered with a cloak and wearing a mask. In his procession around the town he is attended by a number of dancers and in one instance 'dies' and is brought back to life again. In another instance the horse merely perambulates or visits with his attendants and does little or no dancing.

Whitchurch Morris Men performing a mummers' play in 1980. St George has been slain and the mother is calling for a doctor to bring her 'one and only son' to life again.

2
The history of
ritual ceremonial dances

Good luck

The ordinary spectator, seeing these dances, will probably at first be enchanted and enlivened by the vitality of the music. He may ask the meaning of the white handkerchiefs, sticks and bells in the morris, or the meaning of the figures and display of the knot in the sword dance, or the meaning of the hobby horse or 'animal man', or the meaning of the attendant 'funny' characters. Often, when asked, most of the dancers themselves will be at a loss to explain the meaning of what they are doing, hinting vaguely at bringing good luck or being part of a fertility ritual. In these answers they would not be far wrong. Often experts themselves cannot give an explanation. Written records before the late eighteenth century are scanty and the systematic purging of dances of their pagan religious content by Christian or secular powers has not helped matters.

First studies will show that English ritual ceremonial dances do not exist in isolation but are part of an extensive and varied, indeed world-wide, culture. One can for example see similarities to Cotswold morris in dances from the Basque country, Tunisia or Iran; the long sword dance in the Shetlands (Papa Stour), Belgium, Germany, former Czechoslovakia, Spain, Italy and even Japan; and examples of hobby-horse dancing in Europe and South America. One realises that the ritual ceremonial dances of England are part of a much wider, but especially European, culture. This is why comparisons with similar surviving dances elsewhere are so interesting. Thus we find many common features of ritual ceremonial dancing throughout the world. For example, these dances are almost all exclusively danced by men and they are all pre-Christian in derivation. In some parts of Africa the ritual dance is still an integral part of tribal custom and in India and elsewhere in Asia the dances still continue with their religious content. In Europe many dances and customs still display striking elements of pre-Christian belief. Finally, all ritual ceremonial dances seem to have three features in common: they consist of perambulations or visitations from place to place at certain times of the year; their purpose is to bring good luck; and in all of them the performers are disguised in some way or other, and if the disguise is broken the luck is broken.

Earliest references

Various forms of chain dance preceded the morris and linked sword dances and the earliest chain dance known is seen in a rock carving in a valley north-east of Luxor in Upper Egypt dating from about 3400 BC. The carving shows seven girls holding hands, every two looking at each other. Ceramic art from Elam shows nine women in a chain, about 3000 to 2600 BC. From then until the birth of Christ there are at least sixty more examples of chain dance, often the sex being impossible to determine.

Written evidence first comes from Greek and Latin authors, who often wrote of the priestly dancing motherhoods like the Daktyles on Mount Ida and the Korybantes and Kuretes in the Dictean cave. Their job was to call in the spring. Clashing swords against shields and making other noises were a means of expelling winter and its attendant evils. Leaping was performed to shake mother earth, skipping to make the crops grow, jumping to make tall corn. Thudding the earth with sticks and clashing of bells were all part of the act and all have their modern parallels in today's morris and sword dances.

And what of the action of the sword dance itself? At one time there existed throughout civilisation the rite whereby a divine king met his death at the end of a prescribed cycle of years. It is now almost wholly accepted that the sword dance is descended from a rite depicting, in stylised form, the end of a divine king. This is what happens in many of the long sword dances like the one at Grenoside, where the captain is symbolically decapitated by having his cap knocked off, or at Greatham in the mummers' play which is part of the dance.

The most remarkable description of ritual ceremonial dancing is of that of the Salian priests of ancient Rome and it is remarkable because of the parallel characteristics that one can see in modern sword or morris dances. The Salian priests were a dancing brotherhood far older than the Rome through which they processed and danced at certain times of the year. Its birthplace was Tibur (Tivoli), one of the oldest dwelling sites of ancient Rome. Later many cities possessed Salian colleges but they pre-dated Imperial Rome and, according to Dionysus, had a direct link with the even older dancing brotherhoods of ancient Greece. The Salians came out each year on 1st March, the old Roman New Year's Day, and on nine other days, processing from station or altar to station, carrying shields or drumsticks which were tapped to the rhythm of chanted verses, gracefully but vigorously executing certain shifting dance figures in quick and recurring tempo (Plutarch). They always attended the Mamuralia, a scapegoat ceremony centred on a man in skins representing the old year and its evils and Anna Perenna, the perennial or new year and its hopes. The outstanding Flemish composer Lassus (1532-94) records seeing such a happening on his visit to Rome about the middle of the sixteenth century and it inspired him to compose (or collect?) a number of *Moresques*. What can we derive from this? That our European morris and sword dances are but different descendants from earlier dance ceremonials, from which were also descended the Salians and the Kuretes, which in their turn were also descendants of some earlier religious ceremonial, all showing these common characteristics: perambulation, bringing of good luck, disguise? All survived in some form or other because they were beloved by the ordinary people and because they were nearer to them and more understandable than newer official religions.

Horses and masks

Another ritual ceremonial always loved by the people was the hobby-horse and other animal masks. The earliest animal masks in historical references are the stag, the horse and the calf, all old figures of Saturnalia, which changed into Carnival. They came out during Carnival from the twelve days of Christmas to anything up to Shrove-tide or Lent, some even in spring or May. The church disapproved of course and the people loved them all the more. The general rule was that before the church reprimands they appeared in midwinter during their twelve days' leave from the underworld. Sometimes the church had them moved to coincide with patron saint feast-days. We first hear of a stag from the Bishop of Barcelona, AD 370, and in AD 636 Saint Isidor of Seville wrote of Spanish pagans who dressed up as beasts. A calf first appears on an Iberian vase in 200 BC and the horse is first heard of in Saint Augustine's well-known sermon of AD 400 in which he reprimands those in the habit of dressing up as horses.

After this there are references all through history to the animal mask. In England the hobby-horse is very much alive still at Padstow and Minehead celebrating the coming of spring. And throughout all the written references 'we cannot fail to perceive in all the animal guisers bringers in of fertility at the turn of the year. Their play invariably exhibits the obscenity proper to the seasonal rite. Obscenity is good fertility magic. The two legged masks who squeak and gibber in the streets are the returned souls...' (V. Alford, 'Hobby Horses', *Folklore,* volume 70, summer 1968). In modern times in England the hobby or hooded horse or some other beast is often to be seen with the modern revival morris team. Its appearance, however, still has on modern audiences the same effect, evoking genuine alarm and terror in young children and grown-ups alike – a weird two-legged beast with human feet which snaps and bites.

A hooden horse attached to the Whitchurch Morris Men. Compare this with the hobby-horses on pages 25 and 26.

What does it all mean?

After all this, the man in the street will still ask about the trappings and the characters in the morris and sword dance. The answer must still be that no one knows for sure. Many theories have been advanced and each time somewhere there is an exception to the rule. The whiteness of the handkerchiefs and shirts in the morris could symbolise purity; the stick dances which sometimes characterise a fight could symbolise a struggle between the forces of good and evil or sometimes when banging the ground they could be stirring mother earth into action. We have already mentioned the black and white horns at Abbots Bromley and there seems to be a contest there too. The morris bells jangle and frighten away the 'evil spirits'. The ribbons sometimes tied through the holes at the tips of the long swords are descended from the banners displayed in those early priestly processions as described by Greek and Roman authors. The morris fool always seems to direct his fooling against somebody in the crowd and mock abuse is part of the act. But the fooling in the sword dance consists mainly of patter and nonsense about the dancers. Sometimes the fool wears a conical cap which is identified with the fool or astrologer. So does the clown in the circus. His cap is just another of those long pointed phallic symbols like the cup and the ball, the spear pointed at the ring, the arrow shot at the mark, the church spire. Is the fool a defier of authority, or the vestige of the former head priest, or the divine made manifest? Sometimes he wears a sooty face and, like the chimney sweep, the witch doctor and the black cat, brings good luck because of the black. Maybe the only significance of the sword lock is that it is a good way to cut off the captain's head and although the figures of the sword dance – intertwining without breaking – did signify the unbroken ring of life, perhaps the dancers only used strips of metal or wood because they were the handiest things available. Sometimes the lock of swords when placed on the captain's or fool's or Betsy's head to kill him is a fertility symbol. Sometimes when it is held up high or is rolled around the set like a wheel it becomes a form of sun worship or it may be that the raising of the lock in England is a forgotten gesture of raising a man, which is the more normal European habit: the fool is raised on the lock so that he can use the traditional fool's licence to speak freely. How do we know for sure? Who will ever tell?

All these actions have survived and were at one time naturally accepted because they all signified in some way or other the struggle of life over death. We today cannot perhaps appreciate the importance of these things so much. Sometimes the symbolism even seems disgusting. But we must remember that at one time the continuance of human existence was literally a matter of life and death, of life *over* death.

Strangely enough this 'bringing of good luck' still has some relevance today, though in this scientific age not in the same 'magical' way. No modern morris or sword dancer, for example, is going to pretend for one moment that thumping the ground or clashing the swords will affect next year's harvest. Nevertheless the fact that the appearance of the dancers with their vitality, youthfulness, cleanliness and cheerful music evokes the response 'isn't it nice to think spring's here again' surely signifies that something of the early basic meaning of the dancing is still there.

3
Growth and decline in England

The early settlers

One of the interesting features of ritual ceremonial dancing in England is that particular sorts of dancing seem to occur in particular areas, for example Cotswold morris in Oxfordshire and Gloucestershire, processional morris in Lancashire, Greater Manchester and Cheshire, long sword dancing in Cleveland and Yorkshire, and rapper sword dancing in Tyne and Wear, Northumberland and Durham. There were other sorts of dancing, too, of which little or no trace remains except for old individual dancers, for example border morris in the counties bordering Wales, molly dancing in East Anglia, a particular sort of processional morris in Derbyshire, morris dancing in the Forest of Dean, Gloucestershire, and hobby horses in East Kent.

There is now little doubt that these regional differences coincide with particular areas of settlement of England, after the departure of the Romans, by Celts, Jutes, Angles, Saxons and Scandinavians. Each wave of settlers brought their own inherited interpretation of the ritual ceremonial dance and it is vestiges of these that have come down to us today. Much research remains to be done, for example on influences from overseas or on the dividing lines between each area of settlement, which sometimes appear blurred or inconsistent with the dances found there, but one can safely say that ritual dancing in England is as old as the first permanent settlers. For example, the rapper or short sword dances are all found in the old kingdom of Northumbria (settled by Norwegian Scandinavians) while the long sword dances are all found in the old kingdoms of York (settled by Danish Scandinavians). The Cotswold morris dances are all found in the territories which were predominantly Saxon. The theory, which one still hears from time to time, that morris dancing was brought to England by John of Gaunt's troops who had learnt it from the Moors – the word 'morris' supposedly being a corruption of 'Moorish' – now no longer holds water. Indeed the word 'morris', which often used to be applied to many sorts of ritual dancing and to some other sporting activities as well, still awaits proper explanation.

Whitsun ales

Where we see traditional morris or sword dancing as it has come down to us today we must remember that these are but vestiges of once far more elaborate annual procession and carnival ceremonials for each community. The emphasis at one time was on the ceremonial rather than on the dancing but in most cases all that has survived is the dancing with one or two attendant characters. There are for example many written references to the Whitsun ales in Cotswold villages in which an elaborate procession still featured largely and which would consist of some or all of the following: village games, the hoisting of the maypole, the choosing of the lord and lady of the May, the wooden horse on which people rode or paid a forfeit, the setting up of a green bower or bar for the sale of specially brewed ale, a feast in a local barn, the carrying of a specially baked cake, the procession of morris dancers, and the procession of various other characters like a jack-in-the-green or a fantastically dressed fool or a man-woman or a Robin Hood or other popular characters. All these are stock characters and appear in most carnival events in England and other countries. One of the most famous recorded ales was the **Kirtlington** (north of Oxford and recently revived) Lamb Ale where a lamb decorated with ribbons used to be carried around the village and later slaughtered and made into pies. Later from the seventeenth to early nineteenth centuries these festivities became more important for their games and pastimes and money-raising for the parish. A Captain Dover started his own 'Olympick Games' on what is now Dover's Hill near Chipping Campden in about 1605. To this many of the local morris teams used to come. During the nineteenth century most of these Cotswold revelries died out, partly because of declining interest by the local communities and partly because of 'disorderliness'.

Rushcart ceremonials

In north-west England the morris dancing used to be a particular part of the annual rushcart procession to the church at the annual wakes holiday in late summer. The bringing of rushes to floor the church for the ensuing winter used to be the occasion for the procession and the annual wakes holiday used to be the occasion for merrymaking, games and other revelries. At one time the annual ceremonials probably took place in May as elsewhere but in this part of the country were moved to late summer because of the climate. Eventually the rushcart ceremonials died out as churches were floored over, and the local wakes holidays became less important as local events as people, using the new railways, went to the new seaside resorts for their annual holidays. At **Saddleworth** (to the east of Oldham in Lancashire) the rushbearing or wake has recently been revived and occurs just before August Bank Holiday, although the exact date varies from year to year. About two hundred dancers from all traditions take part in the Saturday procession.   There are other rushcart ceremonials at **Gorton, Rochdale** and **Whitworth,** all in Lancashire, and at **Sowerby Bridge** in West Yorkshire.

Saddleworth rushcart procession with Saddleworth Morris Men, Lancashire. Note the character perched perilously on the rushcart along with the boughs of wood.

Elsewhere in northern England the sword dancing used to be part of large midwinter processions of mummers and other characters, sometimes called 'guisers', visiting households and farmsteads in the community. In most cases all that has survived is the sword dancing, sometimes with a calling-on song where the captain or leader introduces in song each dancer in turn. All that has survived of the large procession of characters is the Tommy and Betsy.

The nineteenth century

The heyday for morris and sword dancing in England was the early nineteenth century. In the Cotswolds there used, for example, to be much rivalry between villages as to who could turn out the best-dressed teams with the best versions of the dances, or the best new dance to the latest popular tune. At the Kirtlington Lamb Ale the morris teams used to come once a year to compete for the two prizes, 'the ribbons and the cake'. Practices in some teams used to be held throughout the winter months or in others just the week before Whitsun. It was an honour to be chosen for the team. Probably the shape, steps and character of most of the dances done today date from this period of artistic creation in the morris. Competitions between sword-dance teams in the north-east of England lasted well into the twentieth century. Apart from the spirit of competition, the motivation for dancing would be the collection of money and some teams would travel as far as London or the seaside towns to make a ready penny. Other than that, there was undoubtedly much fun and satisfaction to be found in working at and perfecting the dancing. For many it was their only athletic outlet.

Already, however, the decline was nearing. With the quickening pace of the Industrial Revolution after about 1820 and with the growth of new towns, the economic importance of the countryside and of the towns and villages where the festivities were held was being supplanted. Although no English county lost population until after about 1860 there was a gradual shift of population density, and although many festivities had existed in large towns in the previous century, they did not transplant into the new towns in the nineteenth. Gradually the popularity of the Whitsun ales in the Cotswolds declined and the last Kirtlington Ale was held in 1858 and the last of Dover's Games in 1852. Inevitably, as a symptom of declining interest from a declining community, drunkenness and rowdyism set in and this was an additional reason for the ending of many of the festivities.

Elsewhere long sword dancing survived the strongest in the Cleveland Hills area after the local ironstone deposits became important to British steel-making in the second half of the nineteenth century and some of the agricultural villages took on a new lease of life. In Northumberland and Durham the rapper sword-dance teams survived mostly in the mining villages which depended for their existence on the booming coal trade. In north-west England the Industrial Revolution came to the villages and to the village craftsman, who became the industrial worker, and for a time local traditions and customs enjoyed a revival. But gradually in Lancashire and Cheshire, even though the morris teams survived the ending of the rushcart processionals, it was the increase in travelling away for holidays in Wakes Week and the emptying of the towns that led to their eventual decline. Popular tastes were changing and for many the old dances simply lacked appeal. And so it was that from a state of strong and active existence at the beginning of the century, by the end of it much traditional morris dancing was moribund or had died out. The rapper sword dancing in north-east England and the processional morris in the north-west alone remained active into the twentieth century. At this point, thanks to the work of folk music collectors, people in urban communities began to take an interest in the dances again.

4
Where to see traditional teams

There are to be seen in England today many teams of ritual ceremonial dancers – morris dancers or sword dancers – who can claim an unbroken or almost unbroken link with the past. Admittedly the number is small (about fifteen) when compared with the number of teams (about 250) that were in existence about 1800, a date which for many represented their heyday. The encouraging part of the story, however, is that many new teams of young morris and sword dancers have come into existence in all parts of the country and have learnt from the older dancers where they were still alive or in some parts have revived ceremonial dances which belonged to a particular town or area. In this way, therefore, allowing for a break of a few decades and allowing for the inevitable shift of economic activity from rural to urban communities, the tradition of ritual ceremonial dancing in England can be said to be still very much alive. The following are the traditional dance teams that can still be seen performing regularly in England.

Cotswold morris

Bampton, Oxfordshire, lies about fifteen miles west of Oxford and here, by tradition, the Bampton morris dancers dance around the streets and gardens of the village once a year on Spring Bank Holiday Monday (formerly Whit Monday). They are dressed in white shirts, white trousers, white waistcoats, bowler hats with ribbons and flowers and pads of bells and ribbons below the knees. They are accompanied by a fiddler or a melodeon player, a 'fool' or clown carrying a pig's bladder, and a cake impaled on a sword. Members of the audience are invited to take a morsel of the cake for good luck. There are three sides and this tradition can claim an unbroken link with the past. Although the Spring Bank Holiday Monday is their main day for dancing they are to be seen as well on many other occasions throughout the year.

Headington, Oxfordshire, is now a suburb of Oxford, about two and a half miles from the city centre. The morris team here really belongs to Headington Quarry, as distinct from Headington village, and many of the members of the

Arnold Woodley, fiddle player of one of the three Bampton morris sides. He has been playing for the team since the end of the Second World War.

Bampton Morris Dancers, Oxfordshire, dancing on the lawn of a private house in Bampton. The tour from house to house, with refreshments usually provided, is an essential feature of their traditional dancing day.

The Headington Quarry Morris Men, Oxfordshire, performing a stick dance. Accompanying them on concertina is the Reverend Kenneth Loveless, who has been honourably associated with the team for many years.

older teams were in the building trade, particularly its most famous member, William Kimber, who died in 1961. This team also dances regularly by tradition on Spring Bank Holiday Monday around the immediate locality. They are dressed in white shirts, white trousers, blue caps, red and blue crossed baldricks and bells and ribbons at the knees. They are usually accompanied by an accordion player and a 'fool' wearing a smock and odd-coloured socks, and carrying a bladder and an animal's tail. They, too, dance in public on many other occasions throughout the year. At the end of the nineteenth century the team nearly died out but, encouraged by Percy Manning, the antiquary from Oxford University, they kept going until about 1914. Between the wars Quarry men learnt at the local school but until 1948 danced as Oxford City. The present side started in 1949. They also perform a mummers' play and have a sword-dance team.

Abingdon, Oxfordshire, lies seven miles to the south of Oxford. The two morris teams here, Abingdon Traditional and Mr Hemmings Abingdon Traditional, are closely linked

The Abingdon Morris Men bearing the newly elected 'Mayor' of Ock Street, who in his turn is proudly carrying his instruments of office, a sword and a collecting box.

to the Mock Mayor making on the Saturday nearest 19th June each year. What happens at Abingdon is one of the few surviving examples of the election by a community of a May Queen or a Lord of Misrule or Mock Mayor and in Abingdon it was the last who presided over the former May festivities. Now he presides over the day's morris dancing, carrying the team's cup and sword. An ox head on a pole borne by another man also features prominently in the Abingdon dances. It bears the date 1700 and it is this head which gave its name to Ock Street and the 'mayor' is known as the Mayor of Ock Street. The ox head is believed to symbolise the gift of a local farmer who gave the town a large ox for their celebrations. The mayor has always traditionally been chosen from among the morris men and seems to have come from just a few families within the morris dancers. If no candidate stands for election then the mayor of the previous year is re-elected. The dancers dress in white trousers and white shirts, green baldricks with a yellow centre stripe, coloured belts and decorated top hats. This costume dates from the visit of the Queen in 1956. Morris men from Abingdon were reported at Richmond in 1783 but the earliest written record of this team is in the local church records of 1560.

Chipping Campden, Gloucestershire, is about ten miles south of Stratford-upon-Avon and has a traditional morris team. Their traditional dancing day is Skuttlebrook Wake, the weekend after Whitsun. They dress in white with red-spotted 'chokers' and rosettes pinned to their shirts. The earliest exact reference to morris dancing in the locality of the town is 1772.

The late 1970s onwards saw a revival in morris dancing in several traditional villages. New men's teams now dance at **Bidford-on-Avon**, Warwickshire, on Trinity Monday (based

Chipping Campden Morris Dancers, Gloucestershire, accompanied by their hobby-horse and fool with pig's bladder. The photograph captures well the beautiful loose-flowing arm and leg movements.

Hobby-horse and musician with Ilmington Morris Men from Warwickshire. The dancers in the left of the picture are from another team. The hobby-horse (as distinct from the hooden horse on page 13) is probably a late nineteenth-century antiquarian attachment to the morris – the older teams like Headington and Bampton have fools with bladders as their main characters.

on written sources and local information), **Adderbury**, Oxfordshire (written sources and some invention), **Brackley**, Northamptonshire (written sources and a surviving dancer who last danced in 1923), **Bucknell**, Oxfordshire (written sources – a women's side), **Ducklington**, Oxfordshire (written sources and some invention), **Eynsham**, Oxfordshire (mostly local information), **Ilmington,** Warwickshire (written sources, some local information and some invention), **Kirtlington**, Oxfordshire (some written sources, mostly invention), **Lichfield**, Staffordshire (written sources), **Sherborne**, Gloucestershire (written sources and a little invention), **Wheatley**, Oxfordshire (written sources and some invention), and **Winster**, Derbyshire (local information). The Winster tradition is particularly interesting since it has two files of male dancers, a 'gents' and a 'ladies', the latter distinguished by flowered hats. These are clearly visible in the picture on the front cover of this book.

Processional morris

Bacup in Lancashire boasts a team of traditional processional dancers, namely the **Britannia Coconut Dancers** or the 'Britannia Nutters'. They dance around the streets of Britannia and Bacup every year throughout the Saturday before Easter. They are also much in demand at many other events throughout England during the rest of the year. Completely disguised with their blackened faces and dressed in red and white barrel skirts over black breeches, and with the clatter of their decorated dancing clogs, they are one of the more exciting scenes of ritual dancing to be seen in England. The eight dancers are accompanied by a brass band and a 'whipper-in' with a whip whose job it is to clear a space for the team. Originally his job was to drive away evil forces and he is obviously part of a large family of similar characters in almost all ritual folk customs who serve a like function. Their dance varies from a simple procession to two set dances, one performed with the tops of cotton bobbins, called 'coconuts', the other with garlands. The garland dance has roots going far back into history and has obvious connections with the yearly renewal of life in the spring, a theme that is repeated at

Eynsham Morris Men, Oxfordshire. The brown corduroy trousers, smock-type shirts, single wide sashes and top hats are an accurate re-creation of the original dress.

The Britannia Coconut Dancers performing their 'nut' dance at Bacup in Lancashire on an Easter Saturday. The 'nuts' (the tops of cotton bobbins) are attached to the hands and knees.

Helston and at the early morning garland procession at Bampton and in the many garland social dances of northern Europe. The actual figure of the Bacup garland dance seems however to reflect a late nineteenth-century Lancers. The Britannia men can claim an unbroken history in spite of changed circumstances: some of the tunes played by the band are derived from folk songs and some from popular tunes, like polkas of the nineteenth century.

Manley, near Chester, Cheshire, has a team of traditional processional male morris dancers who are particularly active in that part of England but who are also to be seen at festivals and similar events throughout the country. Their dress is white shirts, black breeches with golden decoration down the sides, white stockings, iron-soled dancing clogs, flowered bowler hats, blue and red sashes, a yellow cummerbund and long bead necklaces. They seem to be the epitome of the processional north-west morris. They are accompanied by a concertina band and a side drummer and they trace their origins back to 1934 when a Mr Bob McDermott came to Manley from Oldham in Lancashire to teach the dance which he had performed since he was a boy in the 1890s. In this respect the team are the heirs of Lancashire morris and were not really influenced by the revival. From the very beginning they practised to concertina music. The team kept going until 1942 and was then revived in 1951 through the indomitable efforts of Leslie and Dorothea Haworth.

Linked sword dances

Grenoside, South Yorkshire, four miles north of Sheffield, has a team of sword dancers who appear traditionally on Boxing Day morning (once only), as part of the formerly more elaborate midwinter rituals. The six dancers carry 'swords' about three feet long and, linked together, perform various interweaving figures. The highlight of the dance is the 'decapitation' of the captain, representing the ritual death of the leader of the community who in ancient times was 'sacrificed' for the common good but who came back to life again. At Grenoside the captain is a seventh man wearing a rabbitskin cap with the animal's head to the front. At one point in the dance the captain stands inside the circle of six dancers, known as his 'sons', the swords are locked around his head and then drawn. The captain falls over and the cap is knocked off. The dance carries on but the captain comes back to life again. The clog-dance step which forms part of the dancing has connections with the solo clog dancing still found occasionally in country districts. The Grenoside dancers are dressed in red decorated jackets, black caps and white trousers with a red stripe. Although the team twice nearly died out

Manley Morris Dancers in Cheshire performing a dance figure known as 'All in a row'. Note the musicians – a band of concertinas only – accompanied by a big bass drum.

Grenoside Sword Dancers, South Yorkshire. The lock has been formed over the captain's head and when it is 'drawn' his cap will be knocked off and he will roll over as if symbolically decapitated. The thriller writer, Ngaio Marsh, used the idea in one of her books, 'Off with his Head'.

because of two world wars, it managed to revive in 1922 and 1947 and the present team maintains strong links with the past.

Handsworth, South Yorkshire, is also near Sheffield, about three miles south-east of the city. There is a team of eight traditional sword dancers who have continuous links with past teams and who have recently revived the custom of dancing on Boxing Day morning. They do a short tour of three or four stops locally, ending up at Handsworth. Recently they have branched out from the linked sword dance and have started to dance Cotswold morris as well. They have also revived the local version of the Derby Ram, 't'Owd Tup', a sort of mumming play. As sword dancers they wear a very striking uniform of black military-style short jacket with silver facings, maroon caps, white trousers and black leather gaiters. Again, as with many others, this team did not dance during the Second World War but got together again shortly afterwards with six of the original dancers. Records of the older teams go back to 1888 but obviously the tradition is very much older than this.

Loftus, Cleveland, is between Whitby and Saltburn. The

Handsworth Traditional Sword Dancers, near Sheffield, displaying a perfect eight-man sword lock. Note the military-style jackets and forage caps.

sword-dance team here is the most active guardian of the well-known tradition of linked sword dancing centred on the distinctive Cleveland area. Although they no longer appear on a traditional dancing day they make many appearances at local events and shows and also at large festivals like Llangollen and Tees-side, where they have won prizes. They also make occasional trips to Europe. Earliest records of the team go back to the 1890s although again the tradition here is obviously much older than this. A team continued in almost permanent existence until 1931 and then died out. Another team was started in 1950, as part of the forthcoming Festival of Britain celebrations, made up of boys from the local secondary school, and this link has continued ever since with new members of the team being recruited from the school. The Loftus dance has two separate figures, each beginning with an overhead clash of swords and ending with a lock. Many of the figures are said to symbolise distinctive agricultural activities like cutting corn, loading hay or drawing a cart and at the end of the dance an 'old woman' is sometimes 'sacrificed'. The team believes their costume should be social rather than military. and it consists of white trousers and shirts, blue waistcoats and red cummerbunds.

Loftus Sword Dancers, Cleveland, performing a 'single and double over' figure. This shows clearly the difference in choice of dress (social in character) from many of the other long sword dance teams who adopted military-style dress at the beginning of the twentieth century.

Goathland Plough Stots, North Yorkshire, on their traditional dance tour in January. The sword dancers follow the plough, which has been blessed in the local church on Plough Sunday.

Goathland, North Yorkshire, also has a strong team of long sword dancers, the Goathland Plough Stots. They have the capacity to put out three teams, boys, juniors and the senior team, and they regularly travel throughout England. Their traditional appearance starts with the Blessing of the Plough at the local church on the first Sunday after Twelfth Night. (If Twelfth Night is a Sunday then this occurs on the following Sunday.) The dance always occurs on the following Saturday at 9 a.m. (the traditional Plough Monday has been abandoned because the team have to go to work on weekdays). They are also in the process of trying to revive their mummers' play. Another traditional team, **Guisborough**, Cleveland, also appears occasionally for specific local events and teams from **Kirkby Malzeard**, North Yorkshire, and **Ampleforth**, North Yorkshire, have been revived.

All the dances in this area, including Loftus, are closely related. Sometimes a team was started as a breakaway from another, and to the outsider they all appear very similar. At one time between the two world wars the North Skelton team was known as the 'queen of the long sword' because of the high standard of performance. Invariably when the teams do appear they are accompanied by their traditional fool or 'Betsy'.

A considerable distance away, but obviously connected, is a fishermen's long sword-dance team at **Flamborough**, just to the north of Bridlington, Humberside. This team too, gets together and performs on occasions, sometimes even on a Boxing Day, and there exists a photograph of a boys' team dancing outside the Ship Hotel in 1964. The dance here is an interesting variant of the other long sword dances. Although the figures are very similar, there are eight dancers instead of six and they are dressed in blue woollen jumpers and caps and white trousers. Moreover, they dance with wooden laths instead of 'swords' and this, and the fact that these are held in the left hand instead of the right, indicates that they represent implements used in making or repairing nets. The process of weaving or 'threedling' the nets is represented in the figures of the dance.

High Spen, Tyne and Wear, is about six miles south-west of Newcastle upon Tyne and boasts a team of traditional rapper sword dancers, the High Spen Blue Diamonds. They rank the title of 'traditional' because today's team of young dancers is directly descended from the team founded in 1926 by Fred Forster (1893-1964). Fred himself, and his brother-in-law, had danced with an earlier local team, the Vernon Troupe. At the end of the nineteenth century rapper dancing was a common sight in the coal-mining villages of Northumberland and Durham, especially at Christmas time. Their rapper dance is particularly associated with Tyneside pit villages (Fred Forster himself was a pitman) and seems to have evolved in the eighteenth century, probably from the older long sword dance, but with a much shorter more flexible sword with a handle at both ends, one of which swivels. The dance is nearly always preceded by a calling-on song which was introduced in the first half of the nineteenth century. The actions are faster and closer-knit than the long sword dance and have the added distinction of fast tap stepping, or 'jigging', performed to fastish tunes in 6/8 time (probably a twentieth-century development). Each village evolved its own variations of the figures and the stepping. The older village teams were certainly spurred on by the prevalence of competitions in nearly every activity in this part of England, from leek growing to rapper sword dancing. Whereas both the long sword and the morris dances have their parallels throughout northern Europe, there is nothing quite like the rapper sword dance anywhere else, especially when performed by dancers who have built up their team experience to a high pitch of excellence. The High Spen team dance with their traditional characters, a Tommy and a Betty (both male). The dress consists of white shirts, royal blue

High Spen Blue Diamonds photographed in 1988. Note the six-sword lock, which must have been made with the 'Betsy' joining in. Also note the 'hoggers' or knee breeches loose at the knee.

'hoggers' (knee breeches loose at the knee), navy blue tie, navy blue socks and a light blue sash. The team have danced at many festivals and competitions throughout England but prefer 'local events to national prestige events: it keeps us in touch with our roots'. The team has no particular dancing-out day but they do hold a weekend long 'mini-festival' about the middle of May each year.

Until a few years ago another traditional team at **Earsdon**, Tyne and Wear, about seven miles north-east of Newcastle, the Royal Earsdon Sword Dancers, were active but seem now to be in abeyance. One can only hope that this fine traditional team, which earned its prefix after a command performance before Edward VII at Alnwick Castle, will one day be revived by local people.

Hobby-horse dances

Padstow, Cornwall, is on the north coast of the peninsula at the mouth of the river Camel. On 1st May one of the best-known folk customs in England, the 'Old Oss' ceremony, takes place in the town. The 'Oss' (which is a hobby-horse carried by a man on his shoulders, his head covered by a grotesque mask) is kept in the stables of the Golden Lion inn and he comes out every year on May Day to dispense his 'magic'. The ceremony starts at midnight on 30th April when

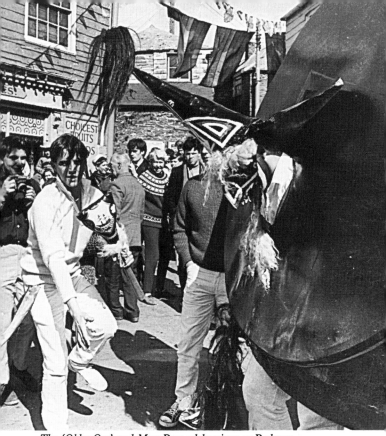

The 'Obby Oss' and May Day celebrations at Padstow.

the 'mayers', who attend the 'Oss', go round the town summoning by song the chief citizens of the town to their bedroom windows. Very early the next morning these mayers are out in the surrounding woods cutting fresh may boughs with which to decorate the streets. At noon the 'Oss' is summoned from the stables and he comes out to dance throughout the day through the streets attended by a large crowd, which includes the musicians playing the haunting May Day melody, the mayers, and a 'teaser' who dances before the 'Oss' with a ceremonial club. At one time the canvas body of the 'Oss' was covered with wet tar and it was believed to be lucky for a girl to be caught under his skirts and receive tar stains on her face or clothes. This certainly meant marriage before 1st May next year. From time to time the 'Oss' sinks to the ground apparently dead but then at a compelling moment in the song leaps to life again. Any visitor to the town on this day cannot fail to be moved by the music, the dancing and the occasion. To local people it is one of the most important events of the year and to some local girls being caught by the horse is significant. There are now three 'Osses' at Padstow: the original 'Obby Oss', the Blue Ribbon 'Oss' which dances in friendly rivalry, and a children's 'Oss'.

Minehead, Somerset, is on the coast and has two hobby-horses which perambulate the locality between 30th April and 3rd May. The first was at one time owned by fishermen and seafarers living on the quay and is known as the Sailor's Horse or Quay Horse. The other, the Town Horse, has had many owners and, according to where the present owner lives, is known by that district. For example, if the owner lives in Alcombe, then the horse is known as the Alcombe Horse. Both horses look much the same and consist of a heavy wooden frame covered with hessian and hundreds of brightly coloured strips of material. The man inside is completely concealed by a grotesque mask. Both are accompanied by a musician and a drummer but the Town Horse is accompanied in addition by four Gullivers or 'mummies' also dressed up in hessian and brightly coloured material. Their masks are even more grotesque than the horse's. As the little party proceeds around the town 'victims' are seized from among the audience by the Gullivers, held in a horizontal position by two of them, and 'booted' by the front of the horse ten times. On the last night the 'victim' holds hands with the horse for a short dance or, if a girl, is now taken under the horse's skirt for the dance-around. The two horses perambulate the town, occasionally meeting in friendly rivalry, but between the two world wars the rivalry became more intense and it became traditional for the two groups to fight until each horse was smashed. The ceremony starts at Whitecross on 1st May at 6 a.m., when both horses attend a short prayer, and ends before 10 p.m. at Cher, both places where local men were killed during Danish raids many centuries ago. During the festivities the two horses visit **Dunster**, which used to have its own horse known as Black Devil, similar to the Padstow hobby-horse. It is resurrected now and again and resembles the Minehead horses in design.

Combe Martin, Devon, has seen the revival of an old custom, the Hunting of the Earl of Rone, which used to be a May Day event but is now spread over the later May Bank Holiday with drumming the town on Friday, children's pro-

The Abbots Bromley Horn Dancers, Staffordshire, are accompanied by a jester, a Robin Hood, a Maid Marian, a hobby-horse and two musicians. The white horns are to the left of the picture and the black horns to the right.

cessions on Saturday and the search for the Earl on Sunday. On Monday he is led to the harbour mounted backwards on a donkey. At his capture there assemble a large band, rows of dancers and a Padstow-like hobby-horse. At each pub they shoot the Earl and the hobby-horse dances over the body. At the harbour the Earl is replaced with a dummy that is then thrown out to sea.

Salisbury, Wiltshire, has Hob-nob, a tourney hobby-horse (now kept in the museum) which sometimes processes once a year with the Giant and morris dancers at midsummer on the eve of St John's Day, 23rd June, the festival of the tailors.

Horn dance

Abbots Bromley, Staffordshire, lies midway between Stafford and Burton upon Trent. It is the scene of the well-known horn dance performed traditionally 'on the first Monday after the first Sunday after the fourth of September'. The ceremony does not belong to any of the three categories of ritual ceremonial dance mentioned above. Six dancers in Tudor costume carrying reindeer horns mounted in wooden heads perform a simple processional and set dance throughout the entire village on the appointed day. They visit the streets, the farms and local squire accompanied by a Jester, a Maid Marian, a Robin Hood, a hobby-horse and two musicians, one with a melodeon and one with a triangle. Robin Hood carries a bow and arrow and Maid Marian carries a wooden object which looks like a ladle but is to more knowing eyes a phallic symbol. Three of the horns are black and three are white, possibly denoting the opposing forces of good and evil, and indeed the basis of the dance appears to be a challenge between the two sides and the triumph of good over evil. Nobody knows how old the dance is but it goes back a very long way and its purpose was obviously fertility. The earliest written reference is only 1686 and it is clear that before then the emphasis was on the hobby-horse rather than the horns, of which one set has been carbon dated to AD 1065 ± 80. The horns and costumes are still kept in the local church, for centuries the most practical place in which to keep things belonging to the community. There is a tradition that neither the horns nor the costumes must ever leave the parish and if the dancers perform outside the village they use a duplicate set of horns.

5
Carrying on the tradition - modern teams

Modern Cotswold morris

There are very few men's traditional dance teams left in England now, traditional in the sense that the teams have a continuous or near-continuous connection with the past. Much depends, however, on one's interpretation of 'traditional'. Allowing that the centres of social activity changed as the economic life of the country changed, and that activities that at one time had a rural setting now have an urban setting, then one could say that because many folk-dance and song activities that have started up among younger people in towns and cities draw their inspiration and knowledge from the country, the tradition in England is still very much alive despite a break of a few decades. Thus nearly every large town and city in England has its modern team of morris dancers and there are now well over four hundred such clubs in existence (a full list may be obtained from the Morris Ring or from the Morris Federation, details of which are given in chapter 11).

Many of these teams perform regularly in the open in the summer and often at other times of the year. They concentrate mostly on Cotswold or border morris and have taken great care to learn from traditional sources where possible. They nearly all have traditional characters with them like fools or animals, often of ingenious design. The Beaux of London City team, for example, have a hobby-horse ridden by a London 'bobby' and the Westminster Morris Men have a fine unicorn. About six times a year the teams organise large meetings for morris dancing when up to two hundred dancers come together to give public performances during a weekend. These meetings are organised in turn by different teams acting as host, so that the meetings move around England from year to year.

There is, however, one regular big meeting of morris dancers every year at **Thaxted** in Essex. Here one of the earliest 'revival' teams acts as host and organises dance tours for the visiting teams throughout the surrounding countryside. In recent years this meeting has always been held during the last weekend in May.

Coventry Morris Men performing a rapper sword dance in the ruins of Coventry Cathedral in 1991 – their sixtieth anniversary. They were one of the first of the 'revival' teams and the musician, Bill Cleaver, is a founder member of the team.

Modern processional morris

Many of the new teams of dancers in England concentrate on some of the other types of ritual ceremonial dance which belong to their locality and have taken great care in carrying on a particular tradition. In north-west England there are teams of dancers at **Abram, Clitheroe, Colne, Failsworth, Garstang, Gorton, Horwich, Lancaster, Leyland, Manchester, Preston, Rivington, Saddleworth** and **Whitworth,** all in Lancashire, as a sample example who all concentrate on processional morris as associated with Lancashire. Also notable is **Fosbrook, Stockport,** in Cheshire.

This form of morris presents one of the few instances where ritual ceremonial dancing became part of the annual cycle of events of new industrial communities, in this case based on the cotton industry in the first half of the nineteenth century in north-west England. Although their numbers declined in the second half of the century there were nevertheless up to the time of the First World War at least thirty teams of men dancing regularly. Most of these teams broke up at the out-

Manchester Morris Men. This team was one of the first of the modern revival teams to take an active interest in traditional north-west men's processional morris.

Horwich Prize Medal Morris Men, Lancashire, performing a dance with decorated sticks. Note the clogs, necklaces and caps instead of flowered hats. The musicians are playing a mixture of brass instruments and melodeon.

break of war and made only occasional appearances thereafter, the team at Royton being the most regular. There were,
however, enough of the older dancers left, even up to the
present day, to instruct new teams of dancers on the steps,
dress and music. In their luxuriously decorated hats, broad
coloured sashes and cummerbunds, beads, dark breeches and
decorated dancing clogs, the new teams are as resplendent as
the older ones were and their number has increased rapidly.

Carnival morris

Another sort of morris dancing to be found these days in
north-west England is girls' carnival morris, sometimes called
'fluffy' morris. To many people in this part of the country this
alone is what is meant by the term 'morris dancing'. Carnival
morris is a highly competitive display dance performed by
troupes of about sixteen girls in short skirts to the accompaniment of any suitable music relayed over the public address
system or to the accompaniment of a tambourine. The displays usually take place at local carnivals and fetes stretching
over a wide area from Lancashire down into Cheshire, Derbyshire, Staffordshire and across to north Wales. There must be
a thousand troupes in existence. Many men's morris-dance
teams strenuously deny that carnival morris, being in the
main a girls' morris, has anything to do with what they call
'the real morris'. Nevertheless carnival morris has a proven
continuity and is a living, evolving folk-art form accepted,
understood and fostered by the communities to which it
belongs. It is moreover based on the men's processional
morris of the nineteenth century. After the shock of the First
World War very few of the men's teams met again and in their
absence new troupes arose consisting of young boys and girls.
These troupes were often taught by the older men dancers or
else their dance was based on what they could remember
from seeing the men's dancing. Between 1920 and 1930 the
girls' troupes became the accepted mode and by this time the
dance evolutions were almost entirely their own, bearing very
little resemblance to the original men's dances.

Modern sword dancers

In north-east England and Yorkshire there are new teams of
male dancers who specialise in performing the sword dances
native to their area. For example, a team of sword dancers at
Redcar in Cleveland has revived the long sword dance associated with **Greatham** across the Tees and they perform the
dance outside Greatham church every Boxing Day. The

Redcar team was formed in 1967 to revive the Greatham long sword dance which had last been performed by a schoolboy village team during the 1953 Coronation celebrations. This team had been trained by the village schoolmaster following instructions given by the leader of the pre-1914 teams. The last regular performances were before the First World War and the dance was performed only sporadically thereafter until the mid 1930s. Incidentally, the performance still retains, as part of the dance, a complete mummers' play, believed to be the only surviving example today.

There are other well-established modern sword teams at **Barnsley**, West Yorkshire, and **Spen Valley**, near Cleckheaton, West Yorkshire, which since the 1970s have developed dances and traditions of their own.

The rapper sword dance is performed by teams like the **Stockton on Tees** Blue and Gold Rapper Dancers, who have won many prizes locally, the **Monkseaton** Morris Men, from near Whitley Bay, and the **Newcastle Kingsmen**, the old University side. The Sallyport team (also at Newcastle upon Tyne) has been going since 1969 and has developed its own version of the Newbiggin dance, a quasi-new tradition.

Border morris and molly dancing

Since the mid 1970s there has been a growing awareness of regionally characteristic dances which are thought to be worth reviving. At one time the morris was identified only with the typical Cotswold morris dance but then horizons began to widen. It started first with the north-west processional morris in the 1950s. Nowadays hardly any morris side in the north-west dances Cotswold morris. Further south there has been a revival of border morris of the counties of Shropshire, Herefordshire and Worcestershire with its distinctive dress of rag jackets and blackened faces, first mentioned in 1609. The Silurian Border Morris, based at **Ledbury**, Herefordshire, researched and enquired, and resurrected the dances. The Shropshire Bedlams, around **Craven Arms**, Shropshire, are in the same vein but use their own material. Molly dancers used to be a common sight in East Anglia on Plough Monday (the first Monday after Twelfth Night). Each group of dancers was black-faced, covered in ribbons and had a man-woman, the Molly. In the mid 1970s at **Mepal**, Cambridgeshire, the Molly Men were revived. They dance in and around Mepal on Plough Monday and then on Market Hill in Cambridge. (Molly dancing was last seen in the 1930s at Little Downham, near Ely.) Another event in Cambridge-

Left: The Wychmen from Northampton at the Rickmansworth Canal Festival, May 1993, performing a border morris dance. They are dressed in traditional rag jackets, top hats with pheasants' feathers and clogs. Their faces are blackened for disguise.

Below: Silurian Border Morris Men, Herefordshire, performing at the annual Bromyard Folk Festival. Their faces are blackened and they wear bowler hats and black dress coats.

Shropshire Bedlams, near Craven Arms, Shropshire, performing one of their dramatic stick dances. The dress (rag jackets and top hats) and the disguise (blackened faces and hands) are consistent with the border morris tradition but the dances are of their own devising.

The Seven Champions Molly Dancers, Kent. Strictly speaking, this team is not within the East Anglian tradition but nevertheless has produced its own distinctive and impressive performance.

shire, the **Whittlesey** Straw Bear Festival, with much molly dancing, has been recently revived, and also takes place over the weekend of Plough Monday. Elsewhere many villages used to have a dancing Jack-in-the-Green on 1st May and one has been revived at **Whitstable**, Kent.

The biggest recent change, however, has been the upsurge of women's, and then mixed morris, sides. There is historical evidence of the existence of women's sides not only in ancient times but also from the nineteenth and twentieth centuries, particularly in the north-west of England, where the social structure of the time did not preclude 'ladies' dancing in public. There is today a 'customary dance' for women which takes place at **Great Wishford** in Wiltshire on Oak Apple Day, 29th May.

After the formation of three women's sides in 1973 (**Bath**, **Cardiff** and **England's Glory**) came a whole host of others. It is difficult to underestimate how rapidly the ceremonial dance scene changed thereafter, from the old rigid 'male only' picture. Not all of it has been good, but there is now an

Great Wishford Faggot Dancers from Wiltshire performing their faggot dance outside Salisbury Cathedral. They are dressed in nineteenth-century women field workers' costume as mentioned in the first printed reference to the dance.

Poynton Jemmers, Cheshire, on the arena at the Sidmouth International Festival of Folk Arts, Devon. This is an all-women team who perform either traditional Cheshire dances or material of their own.

immeasurable amount and range of activity to watch and to participate in. Much of it is of a very high quality with good dancing and good music.

At this point it would probably be advisable to compile an up-to-date categorisation of modern ceremonial dance teams as compared with the three major categories described in chapter 1, such has been the burgeoning of research and activity over the past twenty years. Nearly all are performed by all-male teams, mixed teams or all-female teams.

1. *Cotswold morris*: the traditional style of morris from the Cotswold villages. Some teams emulate the slow rhythms and high leaps described by the older morris dancers (see pages 78-80).

2. *North-west morris*: including all the various styles, from Lancashire and the Cheshire Plain, of processional morris.

3. *Border morris*: which has elements of the processional morris.

4. *Molly dancing:* from East Anglia. The number of dancers is sometimes smaller than in the above categories.

5. *Sword dancing*: both long-sword and rapper.

6. *Garland and stave dancing*: mostly performed by teams of women performing precise and often delicate movements.

7. *Hobby-horse dancing.*

Persephone, a women's team from Bradford, West Yorkshire, at the Rickmansworth Canal Festival, May 1993, performing a garland dance. Note the clogs with clusters of bells and the necklaces.

6
The story of the English country dance

The earliest forms

Dancing has always featured as a ritual in tribal custom and primitive religion, in Britain as much as anywhere else, and it is from the ancient rituals of the past that the folk dances of today are derived.

The forms of the dance, which were common all over Europe and are still to be found in some European countries, were the rounds, the farandoles and the heys. According to pictorial evidence all classes joined in these dances on festive occasions, at least up to the beginning of the fourteenth century. All dances were included in the term 'carole', which meant that people sang as they danced. The habit of singing while dancing was never quite lost and there are still instances of singing dances to be found, one of them in the Faroe Islands. However, the introduction and use of instrumental music to accompany the dancing made further developments and new creations in the dance possible.

The farandole was a linked dance with a chain of dancers led by a man choosing his own steps and following a meandering course. It was interrupted at times by certain figures, such as leading the line under an arch made by the first couple. In another figure all the dancers held up their arms to form arches; the leader then led the chain through the arches, each arch in turn collapsing and joining the line until it was straight again. (This still happens in some European and North American dances.) This was a form of hey or figure-of-eight or winding in and out. The true hey occurred when two farandoles met, relaxed hands and threaded through each other, afterwards taking their separate ways. There are many dances in today's English folk-dance repertoire in which the hey or figure-of-eight is the basic characteristic of the dance, as for example in the 'Dashing white sergeant'.

The rounds or, as they were sometimes called, branles (or brawls, but not in the modern sense) were linked dances performed in a circle, sometimes concentrated round some symbolic object such as a green bush, a jack-in-the-green (man dressed as a bush) or a maypole. Variety in the circle could be achieved only by altering the steps and the rhythm

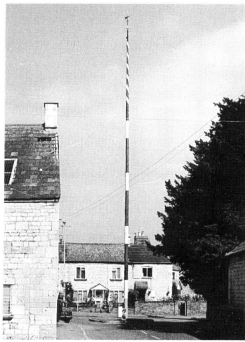

The 90 foot tall maypole at Paganhill, near Stroud, Gloucestershire. It is occasionally renovated as necessary and is still important in a local ceremony in early summer. The very name suggests a place of great antiquity.

or by moving to left or right or in and out. Incidentally, the custom of dancing round the maypole with plaited ribbons, was introduced into England only in 1889 by Professor Ruskin for his student teachers and was thereafter widely used as a suitable form of dancing in schools. Normally the maypole would be hoisted on village greens at the beginning of the spring festivities and would be the centre of some of the old round dances. A 90 foot tall maypole is still to be seen at **Paganhill**, near Stroud in Gloucestershire. It is embellished with flowers every Whit Monday.

Helston – England's oldest dance

Eventually the habit of caroling died out and the haphazard arrangement of dancers of any sex, was replaced by the couple, or alternation of man and woman, as the unit of the dance. In Cornwall the famous Helston Furry Dance is a very old survival of this form of dancing and has very strong ritual undertones. The line of dancers, led by the town band, proceeds around the streets of Helston and sometimes passes in the front door of one house and out at the back, in the back of the next house and out of the front. This is obviously a good luck processional which performs a 'spring cleaning' function, expelling the old spirits of winter and letting in the new of spring. The ceremony takes place every year on 8th May, or the nearest Saturday, 8th May being the feast day of St Michael, patron saint of the parish. There are three processions altogether, the first at 7 a.m. danced by the young boys and girls of the town, the second at noon in formal dress led by the mayor, and the last at 5 p.m. in which everyone joins. It is an honour to be chosen for the mayor's procession but the best time to see the dance is in the early morning before the crowds grow.

The first ballroom dances

As the old dances became more definitely organised into alternations of men and women, so gradually other ideas came in, stimulated by the movement about Europe of the travelling troubadours with their music and dance inventions for fashionable company. The French produced their Basse Danse, a processional dance in which steps were arranged according to rigid rules. Its Italian form was more compact because by this time dancing had moved indoors and was taking place at all times of the year not just at particular occasions at particular times. The simplest form of these new 'ballroom' dances was a dance in file up the room, face about and repeat the steps to original places. Soon simple figures emerged and we had the earliest form of the longways dance.

It is difficult to say who invented what figures and why. Cecil Sharp felt that the big round dances published by Playford in the mid seventeenth century ('Sellenger's Round' and 'Gathering Peascods') were very old and derived from the old rounds and that where those rounds were progressive, that is one couple leading out to the next and gradually working their way round the ring, so that type of progressive dance may have developed into a longways dance. Although the shapes of the dances probably evolved quite simply as people had bright ideas, the longways for six, eight or more couples, the square for four and the square for eight were all known in Italy before they came to England. Eventually the 'longways for as many as will' came to be known as especially English. In fact its first known mention as a technical term was in *Il Balarino* (Garoso, 1581).

What would seem to have happened was a sort of two-way

The Helston Furry Dance, Cornwall. This is the formal dress procession led by the Mayor, who in turn is preceded by the local brass band struggling through a dense crowd.

movement, a process of cross-fertilisation and that is surely the essence of the 'folk process'. The old festive communal dances were, through the influence of the travelling trouba- dours, adopted and adapted for fashionable higher-class cir- cles quite early on and eventually, largely through the influ-

The Helston Furry Dance, Cornwall. This is the children's procession. Even at this early hour, 7 a.m., the crowd is already dense. They are performing the fairly simple two-hand turn figure before resuming the procession.

ence of the Italians, became formal, complex and difficult. Meanwhile ordinary or 'common folk' continued with their old-fashioned rounds, farandoles and heys and probably, but not certainly, also danced some of the latest court dances, or 'measurers' as they were known, as they filtered down to them. Eventually, as often happens, the fashionable world turned to the grass-roots world for fresh inspiration.

Country dances replace court dances

At the end of Elizabeth I's reign there was a growing and noticeable reaction in court circles against the dances so favoured by the Italian dancing masters because they had become too formal. There was instead a growing interest in the dances that the ordinary folk were doing. There are several references to interest taken by the queen herself in their dances, which were already known as 'country dances'; she looked on admiringly from an upstairs window while local villagers or townsfolk danced below, at Warwick in 1572 and at Cowdray in 1591, 1600 and 1602.

A mere look of royal approval was enough and eventually the dancers at court reduced their dances to a more socially acceptable form by building on the foundation of old English country dances. In 1595 we first hear of country dances being performed at court and this marked the beginning of a new era of popular social dancing that was later to affect the whole of northern Europe.

The adoption of country dances was not, however, immediate. Queen Elizabeth had, after all, only watched occasionally, and at the masques or fashionable entertainments the old courtly dances still persisted with just an occasional country dance. The masques were a form of sophisticated domestic entertainment which developed among the nobility during the sixteenth and seventeenth centuries. The dances shown at them were usually performed only by the accomplished, while the rest of the company sat by and watched. Watching is one thing but sometimes it leads to the urge to join in and this is why country dances came so much into vogue as time went on: they were for everyone and in addition were livelier, especially the music (many of the tunes were apparently Irish in origin).

After about 1625 country dances began to penetrate court circles far more. They had probably already been popular lower down the social scale at court and in wealthy homes ever since the previous century, following the more stable times of Henry VIII's reign, particularly among those in the

Illustration from an early eighteenth-century broadsheet. It shows a couple dancing a jig of an unspecified nature.

country. One can imagine the situation: these better-off rural people travelled little, especially in winter, and had to make their own entertainment among a household of men and women servants. Here the lively country dances flourished, having been taken from those local people who happened to be servants of the house. Many dances would be adopted and added to now and then by some outside visitor. That this must have been so is evidenced by the naming of many of these dances after famous country houses or palaces such as Hunsdon, Holmby, Nonesuch, Greenwich, Apley and others.

The merry English

The first ever published collection of English country dances, known as *The English Dancing Master*, was published in 1651 by John Playford, a very successful music seller and publisher in London. The 105 dances and tunes, most of which were probably at least a hundred years old at the time, had been gathered by Playford and others during the period of the Commonwealth and, in his words, contributed 'a tentative offering to the public'. It is not difficult to imagine the relief felt after the English Civil War and its consequent political and social upheavals. Now society entered on a period of dancing, singing and music making. In particular Playford's 'offering' may have been made to the new gentlemen of the Inns of Court (where many of the Revels were normally held), who returned there with the coming of more peaceful times. The tradition of dancing there would have been broken during the war and the new generation would have been ignorant of those forms of dance customary at the Revels, whose return was now eagerly awaited. Playford was probably presenting a record of dancing which had never been the province of the fashionable London dancing master but which was widely practised and known in out-of-town houses.

The first edition of *The English Dancing Master* gained immediate profit and popularity to such an extent that in thirty-five years (that is by 1686) it ran through seven editions, each larger than the one before. John Playford's son, Henry, carried on publication and brought out five more editions while their successor John Young brought out six more making a total of eighteen editions between 1651 and 1728. Nearly all the tunes of the first edition were songs or ballads, many of a much earlier date than the book. By about 1690, however, tunes composed expressly for dancing were becoming more general and in the editions of *The English*

Frontispiece from 'The English Dancing Master', Volume the First, 18th edition, Henry Playford. A longways dance for four couples, with musicians in the minstrels' gallery and polite society looking on. Note the 'safe distance' between the dancing couple: two hands only.

Dancing Master from 1715 to 1728 the song and the dance tunes were equally divided.

As a popular art form becomes more popular, sophistication inevitably creeps in, and so it was with the dances. The first of Playford's editions reflect very much the manner of

Illustration from a mid eighteenth-century broadsheet – a rather romantic view of country dancing, but the musician playing the pipe and tabor is genuine enough.

Engraving by W. Hogarth, 'The Country Dance' or 'The Happy Marriage', 1753. This is obviously a longways dance. Note the minstrels' gallery and the gentlemen's hats piled in one corner.

dancing in the reigns of Elizabeth I and Charles I – a sort of abandoned romp – but the later editions reflect more formal manners in which the dancing master once more came into his own and was again an arbiter of social deportment and manners as well as of steps. But in that time and especially after the Restoration, social life became more public and country dancing spread from court and private house to public assembly rooms where larger numbers of people from the 'middling orders' could join in.

The eighteenth century was the heyday of the English country dance when a proliferation of dance publishers followed Playford and Young, and the English country dance swept into every corner of Europe with the result that vestiges of English dance figures can still be traced in European dances today.

The first in the field after John Playford was Walsh. Many of his dances (published between 1711 and 1750) were exact copies of Playford's. There were no copyright laws at the time and publishers used to use each other's material without compunction. From 1730 publishers of dances became more numerous with Wright, Rutherford, Thompson and Bremner between 1750 and 1775, a host of others like Preston, Skillern,

Cahusac, Campbell, Longman and Broderip from 1775 to 1810.

Fashionable in Europe

Meanwhile the English country dance had become popular abroad. In 1706 Raoul Auger Feuillet, under the patronage of Madame La Dauphine, introduced the English dance to the court of Louis XIV. Feuillet published a selection of country dances, many of these adapted from the Playford collections and including one which was a little like a rock-and-roll dance called '*Jeanne qui saute*' or 'Jumping Joan' to a tune which is now familiar to us as 'Cock o' the north'. Feuillet wrote a thesis on the English country dance which he said was the most popular and beautiful to be found in Europe.

The English country dance became the height of fashion at the French court and from there spread to a great many parts of Europe, including Germany, Sweden, Denmark and Norway. One interesting fact to emerge is that the longways dance, even if it probably originated in Italy, was mainly an English development and, among other things, reappeared in Italy. Here is part of a letter from Horace Walpole to a Richard West from Florence in 1740: 'Then I have danced, good gods how I have danced. The Italians are fond to a degree of our country dances. "Cold and raw" they only know by the tune; "Blowzybella" is almost Italian and "Butter'd peas" is "*Pizelli al buro*".'

By 1810 the English country dance was dominated by the publications of Thomas Wilson but already in his books (1812 and 1821) we find the longways country dance giving way to the newer quadrilles and waltzes which had begun to flow back from Europe. Another book of 23 dances, published by G.M.S. Chivers and called *The Modern Dancing Master* (1822), also reflected the new ideas coming in from Europe. The period 1800 to 1815 was the end of the heyday of the English country dance.

By 1840 the English country dance had almost disappeared from the fashionable ballroom. Gradually it gave way to a reversed wave of fashion from Europe in the form of waltzes, quadrilles (from France), cotillions and eventually the polka. When the polka became the rage the set dances became split up into couple dances and by the end of the nineteenth century the emphasis was all on couple dances. The 'Sir Roger de Coverley' alone maintained a dogged existence through into the twentieth century and something of the set dance persisted in the lancers, although these were derived from the quadrilles. After 1840, therefore, one has to trace the development of the English country dance in the so-called backwaters of social life, in English villages and in the Scottish ballrooms where people were not so rapidly affected by new fashions.

Scottish country dancing

If the country dance died out in the English ballroom it nevertheless carried on in the ballrooms of Scotland. In fact it had taken some time to become established there in the first place. A Major Topham wrote from Edinburgh to his niece in Bath in 1775: 'They sit totally unmoved by the most sprightly airs of an English country dance, but the moment one of those tunes (Scottish reel) is played, up they start animated with a new life and you would imagine they had been bit by a tarantula.' The 'reel' referred to is the term that the Scottish have always used for the figure of eight or hey. The Scottish ladies and gentlemen of the 1770s still preferred their old threesome, foursome, fivesome, sixsome and eightsome (not the modern one) reels. These were the dances country folk were still doing both in England and Scotland, dances descended from the heys or reelings that date from the middle ages.

The first published volume of Scottish country dances did not appear until 1789 when John Bowie of Perth published *A Collection of Strathspeys, Reels and Country Dances*. The Scots eventually gave up their antipathy to country dancing and it flourished in Scotland just as it was dying out in the English ballroom. A typical ballroom guide like Mozart Allen's *Reference Guide to the Ballrooms* (Glasgow, 1880) gives about fifty country dances. At the same time a typical English ballroom guide would give only a few among all the Victorian couple and set dances, 'Sir Roger de Coverley', 'The Haymakers', 'The Tempest', 'The Galopede', 'The Triumph', and 'The Waltz Country Dance' being the most typical. Is it any wonder that country dancing, in many twentieth-century eyes, has come to be regarded as Scottish, although Scottish country dances are not specifically Scottish in form or origin? Moreover, by the time Scottish country dances were appearing in print, ten thousand English country dances had already been published at one time or another, although many of these were repetitions and certainly not all were in print.

English village dancing

We know little of what was happening meanwhile lower

down the social scale in the English village of the nineteenth century. Many of the fashionable country dances had doubtless slid down the social scale and were popular with the middle and lower middle classes. They do not seem to have got much further than that. An interesting observer of the scene was the novelist Thomas Hardy. At one time he played the fiddle at the local country dances in his native Dorset, as had his grandfather and father before him. Many passages in his books reflect his love of the tunes and the dances. One dance in particular, 'The Triumph', figures in his novel *Under the Greenwood Tree* and the film *Far from the Madding Crowd*, based on his novel, depicted very well the type of dancing and the music of the time. Hardy remarked that there was a distinction in the villages between the dancing of farm labourers (mostly the very old reels, heys or step dances) and the dancing of the better off, the squire, his family and friends. Probably the only time when farm labourers and squire danced each other's dances would be at festivals like the annual harvest homes when the whole community would get together. Something of the rumbustiousness of early nineteenth-century village dancing can be gathered from this account by John Keats describing a visit to a Lakeland village in 1818. He had occasion to call in on a village dancing school held at 'The Tun'. The dancing, he writes, was 'no cotillion new from France. No, they kickit and jumpit with mettle extraordinary and whiskit and friskit and toed it and go'd it and twirl'd it, tattooing the floor like mad.'

However, by the end of the nineteenth century the village people were also dancing country dances of an earlier period which eventually reached them, in addition to their very much older reels.

It was from this village dancing as it survived into the twentieth century that we today obtain much of our current repertoire of traditional dancing. But this village dancing was itself subjected to so many outside influences from different sources that by the time the dance collectors of the 1900s started work they were presented with a pastiche of everything that had gone on throughout the nineteenth century.

The parts that went to make up this picture were: the survival of some very ancient reels and circle dances; the survival of some late eighteenth-century 'country' or longways dances; the survival of many of the new formations of set dances mentioned in G.M.S. Chivers's book, *The Modern Dancing Master*, published in 1822 (for example, the Sicilian circle dances); the addition of new longways dances com-

Illustration from a mid eighteenth-century broadsheet with, possibly, the dancing master holding a book. Many dancing masters had specially designed small violins with which to provide musical accompaniment while at the same time teaching the dances.

posed in Scotland, some of which were adopted in England; surviving local versions of popular Victorian couple dances; and surviving versions of the quadrilles, lancers and other Victorian set dances.

All folk dances seem to have been fashionable dances at one time or another and some have survived because they became the favourites of the people at festivities or parties after they had ceased to be fashionable elsewhere. The quickstep and the foxtrot may now be regarded in the same light. In some instances they have already undergone the 'folk process'. Readers should visit the sequence ballroom dancing sessions which are now very popular, especially among senior citizens, to understand this.

The dancing masters

One of the interesting features of village life throughout the nineteenth century was the travelling dancing masters. They continued to be active in Scotland until about 1920 but were also active in England, though not for so long. Their style (and therefore also that of the village dancers) was probably not all that different whether in England or in Scotland. They taught popular ballroom dancing of the era, as they knew it. They have been well described by Dr T.M. Flett in his book *Traditional Dancing in Scotland*. They used to travel from place to place, settling in a village for eight or ten weeks at a time and teaching there on two or three evenings a week. They would hire a local hall or barn or even a stable loft and, since they were usually musicians, provided their own music –

often playing and dancing at the same time. Most confined themselves to a particular circuit so that these days when Scottish people talk of dances from a particular region they are really referring to the specialities of past dancing masters plus a number of folk dances preserved from time immemorial.

We also know a considerable amount about the travelling dancing masters of the northern counties of England, such as Northumberland, Cumbria and Lancashire. We are still looking for evidence of dancing masters in other parts of England for we know they must have existed. In these northern counties we know that step dancing was also taught and that Cumbria, Northumberland and Durham, and Lancashire had their own particular styles of stepping and that the people who did them were very proud of them. Step dancing is still a feature in these northern counties and individuals are still to be found dancing a traditional step dance with clogs. Some have gone on to the stage and it is said that even Fred Astaire learnt some of his steps from a lady step-dance teacher from Durham.

The travelling dancing masters used to teach, besides step

Green Ginger Clog Dancers from Hull performing at the 1992 Whitby Folk Week. The setting is the old Market Place with the Market Hall behind.

dancing, the older traditional dances, some of the not-so-old country dances, some of the new quadrilles like 'La Russe', the lancers, schottisches and other couple dances like 'The Swedish', some of which were imported from Europe and America. Often when the dancing master descended on a village, it was regarded as *the* occasion in the annual local social calendar. Sometimes the school would be closed down especially. Often at the end of the week's instruction there would be a special party where the pupils could show off what they had learnt and where older pupils could come and dance the old favourites. Sometimes the pupils would present a dance specially made up for the occasion by their teacher. The dance 'Durham Rangers', so popular with primary school teachers today, must have originated in this way, as did the Manx dances which used to be popular with dance demonstration teams.

After about 1900 or 1910 fashions in popular entertainment changed even in the villages. The travelling dancing masters gradually died out and the villagers learnt their dances mostly from each other or from what filtered down from the town ballrooms.

Village barn dances

Dancing flourished in the villages for a long time and constituted a lively scene. Many of these events came to be known as 'barn dances'. Here are two eye-witness accounts of dance parties about twenty years apart from each other. The similarities are very marked.

The first description is from H.M. Neville's *A Corner in the North* (Newcastle, 1909): 'The tidings of a coming dance stirs them (the local people) as nothing else will. Very few will decline your invitation and although you will be careful to choose a moonlight night for your ball, you need not think that either darkness, distance or bad weather will prevent the arrival of your guests... The music of our balls is supplied by one of the fiddlers of the district, who is seated on a chair raised aloft upon a table which forms the minstrel's gallery for the time being... And when all have come, and The Master of Ceremonies announces the first dance, what a transformation scene it all is compared with the workaday world which the young people have for a few hours left behind them. There is nobility in all labour but a stranger to our country, looking at our guests taking their partners at the sounds of the first strains of "The Triumph" country dance, would never suppose that these well dressed and well mannered young people represent the real workers of our countryside... The dances which, although not so light and graceful as those of southern counties, are yet wonderfully complicated in their figures and steps...'

The second description is from a letter to *English Dance and Song* (EFDSS, April 1949) written by a Mrs Hall of Newcastle upon Tyne. She describes the parties she had attended at Fairhaugh in 1929. She writes: 'The first dance I attended was in the tiny one-roomed school. This was a great social event, and after an early evening milking the farm people and their families tramped for miles across the hills to be there by 7.30 p.m. The band was composed of local people, whose repertoire, though small, was full of life and vigour, especially the pianist who confined herself to the rhythm only. The dancing was spontaneous and the style easy and natural, but the heavy shoes of the men beating out the rhythm of the Northumbrian stepping made drums quite unnecessary.... The only break was for supper which was all given by the local people and served in the nearest farmhouse kitchen which was about two hundred yards away down a very rough pasture field. Owing to this trek, and to help people in the long walk in the dark over the hills to reach the dance, the choice of date depended on the moon... The programme consisted of "Circassian Circle", "Morpeth Rant", "Corn Rigs", "Drops of Brandy", "Roxburgh Castle", "Call of the Pipes", and "The Spanish Waltz" .... There was a good selection of "old time" dances, also "The Valeta", "St Bernard's Waltz", "Eva Threestep", "Boston Twostep" and an uproarious version of "The Lancers". For our friends from across the Border there was "The Eightsome Reel"... The band played and the dancers danced until, at daybreak, usually about five o'clock, the long trek back to the farms began in order to be there for the morning milking.'

When the collectors of the twentieth-century folk dance revival started turning back to traditional sources for material they found parties like these going on all over England and Scotland. In a few places they still occur. Inevitably the nature of the parties has changed as villages have acquired halls and people have bought cars. It should be noted too that the dance repertoire was never consciously 'folk' or 'non-folk' (or 'English' or 'Scottish' for that matter) as it is in our revivalist functions. Rather it was a mixture of all sorts of things – an old country dance, an old-fashioned version of 'The Lancers', a favourite couple dance, a quickstep – and therefore a genuine continuation of the traditional process.

Village barn dances are still widely held but most of them these days are organised by enthusiasts from the local folk-dance or folk-song club. Although they have no direct link with the past and although the repertoire is usually more self-conscious – one will rarely find a 'modern' dance performed – nevertheless the sense of occasion and of social enjoyment are much the same as in the past. Admittedly the timing of the event is no longer linked to milking time and some people come very long distances in cars, not across the hills by moonlight, but the ages and the types of people who come have not changed.

American dances

Many of the dances practised in modern English folk danc-ing are American in origin. This is because many of the dances in the American tradition are so very similar to English dances and have very close historical links with them, be they longways, circle, or the commonly known square dances.

The oldest in the American tradition is the southern square dance as it developed in the Appalachian Mountains. Many dances in this style were noted down by Cecil Sharp on his collecting trip to the Appalachians in 1917 and 1918 and published in *Country Dance Book V*. He called them 'running sets' although they were really a fast-moving running type of square. When seen by Cecil Sharp they were immediately attractive to him because of their rhythmic qualities. Usually danced with four, or sometimes more, couples in a square formation, the dance, as he saw it, was very fast, performed not to music but to the stampings and clappings of the onlookers and the falsetto voice of the caller. The people of the Appalachians descend from the earliest settlers from Europe and the dances may be based on ancient European dances either as Americanised progressive round dances or as highly localised forms of fashionable quadrilles and lancers. Particularly interesting is the Appalachian step-dancing, in which dancers in England became interested after the visit of an American team to Sidmouth in 1978: there are now some very fine display teams in England. From this stepping comes a term 'hoe-down', now a familiar term for a barn dance or similar event.

Western Square is the type of square dancing that most people in England are familiar with, especially its modern descendants like 'Swanee', 'Hot time in the old town tonight', 'Chinese breakdown' and others. Traditionally people associ-ate Western Square with the patter calling of a caller who

Roughshod Appalachian Dancers from Gloucestershire. Their shoes have metal tips and they are dancing on boards to produce the distinctive off-beat rhythmic sound. Music is provided by the fiddler with his back to the camera.

usually manages to guide the dancers through the main figures primarily by a prompt call. These days in America the Western Square has tended to move on from traditional music and is using popular tunes of the 1930s, 1940s and

1950s. Although some regret this use of modern music, it is nevertheless a perfectly natural process, although the fad for devising ever more complex figures will doubtless have its reaction in time. Originally these dances had grown up among all the later European settlers in America – English, French, German, Scottish, Irish, Danish – as they moved further west than the original settlers, and as their home-grown dances had all gone into the melting pot. This time, however, the dances were all based on that later European quadrille or square fashion which had started in early nineteenth-century France and which had become so popular in Europe after the decline of the English country dance.

Somewhere in between comes the New England longways or contra dance for as many couples in a set as the length of the room can take. These are found, and still very widely practised, in the northernmost of the former English colonies, the New England states of America. Most (probably 90 per cent) of the settlers here, from the early seventeenth to the late eighteenth century, were British in origin, and brought with them the style of dance fashionable at home during that period. Most of the longways dances of the late eighteenth century came with them and underwent a process of alteration. Most of them, however, are very similar to our own late eighteenth-century dances, as are their names – 'Soldier's joy', 'Flowers of Edinburgh', 'The Triumph'. However, 'Petronella' became 'Pat Melior', and 'Pins and needles' or 'Scottish reform' became 'Hull's victory' in honour of Captain Hull, who beat the British navy in an engagement during the war of 1812. As in England there was a tradition of travelling dancing masters or 'callers' which has carried on to the present day, many of whom have composed their own new dances and tunes in the traditional idiom.

The Western Square formed the basis of the great square dance craze in England which followed the visit of the then Princess Elizabeth and Prince Philip to Canada in 1949. They found themselves whisked into a square dance, enjoyed it and enthused over it. Britain swiftly followed suit, assisted here and there by American servicemen stationed there. The craze eventually began to die down and, when King George VI died in 1952 and the whole nation went into mourning, it disappeared. But in that short time it had affected nearly every ballroom in England and had brought many new recruits to the folk-dance world.

7
The modern revival

The revival of interest in English folk dancing in Britain has been the main work of the English Folk Dance and Song Society (EFDSS) and the man who was at the centre of the movement was Cecil Sharp. The Folk Song Society was founded in 1898, the English Folk Dance Society in 1911 and the two merged to form the English Folk Dance and Song Society in 1932.

Paradoxically the real revival was started by the Esperance Girls Club, St Pancras, London, under its leader Miss Mary Neal. This club had been founded in 1895 originally to cater for local working-class girls and boys. In 1905 Mary Neal saw an article by Cecil Sharp in *The Morning Post* about the richness of English folk song. Cecil Sharp was at the time a teacher of music in a London school and for long had been dissatisfied with the preponderance of German music in English education. Believing that 'good strong simple melodies, essentially English in character' were more what was needed for English children, he had from 1902 or 1903 taken an increasing interest in collecting folk songs from traditional singers. Composers like Vaughan Williams, Moeran, Grainger and Butterworth joined in his enthusiasm. This interest in native material, however, was also part of the wider contemporary interest in folk music by modern European composers as typified by Tchaikovsky and Balakirev and later by Bartok and Kodaly. They were interested in rhythms, tonalities and tunes as well as nationalism.

In England there were many who told Sharp that no or very few folk songs still existed but he already had found a rich harvest and in 1903 had been elected on to the committee of the Folk Song Society. The article that Mary Neal saw was part of his campaign to 'set folk song into a mighty flame which would burn once more throughout the land'. Mary Neal asked Cecil Sharp to supply some of the songs for the club, which he promptly did. According to Miss Neal, the girls and boys went 'mad' about the songs and she soon enquired from Sharp about dances to go with the songs.

Sharp then remembered a much earlier encounter when on Boxing Day 1899, quite by chance, he had seen for the first time morris dancing performed by the Headington Quarry Morris Men. Captivated by the tunes and in a state of some

Dancers from Armscote, Warwickshire, performing the longways traditional dance 'Flowers of Edinburgh' at Stratford-upon-Avon in 1912. The team was invited over to Cecil Sharp's first summer school

excitement, he had noted them down from their leader, William Kimber, but apart from that he had not known what to do with them. He now put Mary Neal in touch with William Kimber, with the result that Kimber and his cousin came to London and taught their dances to the girls and boys at the Esperance Club. They in their turn passed the songs and the dances on to affiliated clubs throughout the country

there. They are dancing on the lawn of the old Memorial Theatre. In the background is the river Avon and the fields beyond: this scene has changed remarkably little.

through a large body of specially trained teachers.

In 1907, in association with Herbert MacIlwaine, musical director of the Esperance Club, Sharp devised a dance notation and a book of instructions based on what he had learnt from Kimber in London. This was known as *Morris Book 1.* From then on Sharp began collecting more morris tunes and dances and from 1911 the sword dances as well. These were all published in book form until the outbreak of war in 1914 curtailed his collecting activities and those of others like George Butterworth, the composer, who was killed in the trenches.

It was also thought that the social dance had died out completely, but Sharp and others like the Reverend S. Baring-Gould and Mrs Leather did manage to find some dances in Warwickshire, Herefordshire, Surrey and Devon. These were the dances that went to make up *Country Dance Book I* published in 1909. They were all very simple English country dances as performed in the villages.

Strains, however, had been developing for some time between Sharp and Mary Neal. Neal, obviously something of a realist, believed that the dance should be a living, evolving thing, learned from a traditional dancer in the first place and then passed on in the same way, that is by word of mouth. Written notations should only be used as *aides-mémoires* to steps and figures. They should never be made an unalterable and fixed standard. Sharp was far more exacting, far more 'artistic' in his approach. He criticised Mary Neal for her 'laxity in teaching', for her 'lack of attention to standards of performance'. In truth she was ahead of her time and her less pedantic approach has only recently become accepted by the revival movement. But Sharp had already won the approval of the Board of Education for his work so that from 1909 onwards folk songs and dances gained official recognition as part of the school curriculum. This decision was much deplored by Mary Neal.

In 1909 Sharp had started his own school of morris dancing at the Chelsea Physical Training College and this later became the basis of the English Folk Dance Society established in 1911. At the same time, partly because there did not appear to be any more traditional dances to be found and partly because he was looking for dances which were more artistic and more interesting, he spent many months in the British Museum working through all the Playford volumes of English country dances. In all, between 1911 and 1922, 158 'Playford' dances were re-interpreted and published. These dances constituted the main social dance repertoire of the English Folk Dance Society until after the Second World War. Unfortunately this backward leap in time of about 250 years meant that the traditional process in the social dances of the intervening years was almost completely ignored. As later collectors were to find out, there was indeed much left 'in the field' to be collected in terms both of dances and of music, that is of tunes, of styles of playing and of the instruments used. This process of rediscovery started in Devon and northern England in the 1930s, in the Midlands in the 1950s and in East Anglia in the 1970s. In fairness to Sharp, however, although this 'social recreation' approach is now the most viable one, in his day society would not or could not have accepted anything but the educational approach. The main trouble was that the latter lasted too long.

Sharp's new society grew very rapidly as did the Esperance Morris Guild, but after the First World War the latter was allowed to lapse, thus leaving the field clear for the English Folk Dance Society. Unfortunately many of the men in Sharp's demonstration team were killed in that war and in the ensuing years the society became mainly a women's movement. In 1924 Sharp died and the society and the revival movement suffered as a result. The initial enthusiasm died off; the membership declined. Malcontents criticised the emphasis on the academic approach, the fact that the Society had become mainly attached to school work, to holding classes rather than social functions, and examinations. The movement seemed to have become an activity for experts only, lacking the social impact for which Mary Neal had been aiming.

In the 1920s and 1930s there was, however, a renewed interest by some members in the traditional social dance, its sources, its styles and its music. Collectors sallied forth afresh and found in Cotswold villages and in village barn dances more morris and more social dances. Fresh contacts were made with traditional sword-dance teams still existing in the north-east. Gradually, some members of the society turned towards the traditional styles, as they were then being redis-covered. International contacts emphasised how far the Soci-ety's dancing had diverged from the real tradition, as illus-trated by foreign teams of traditional dancers at the first festival at the Royal Albert Hall in 1932 and the International Folk Dance Festival in Hyde Park in 1935.

It was the Second World War that pushed the English Folk Dance and Song Society towards the traditional social dance, especially the Saturday square dances at Cecil Sharp House in London, established to cater for servicemen on leave or passing through London. At last the way to a popular folk-dance revival was seen. The opportunity came immediately after the war when there was a change in presentation and policy ably led by the society's director, Douglas Kennedy (1893-1988), and his wife Helen. The 'Playford' dances were at last abandoned in favour of the traditional dances; examinations and classes were gradually phased out, and popular social functions took their place, assisted by the adoption of the American style of prompt 'calling'. The introduction of a radio programme 'Everybody Swing' and similar programmes in other regions, the square dance craze of 1949 to 1952, the folk-song revival of the 1960s, and the setting up of many hundreds of new folk-song clubs among a new generation of young people encouraged an interest in folk dance which, after about 1965, brought to the folk-dance revival a new and healthy dimension.

8
Social folk dancing today

Social folk dances are for everyone to enjoy on social or festive occasions, as distinct from the ritual ceremonial dances which are for display purposes and are performed by teams of dancers who have been specially trained. Sometimes social dances are also used for display purposes, having undergone some special arrangement. To distinguish social dances from modern ballroom dances, they are called 'folk' or 'country' dances, denoting that they were being used in rural communities long after they had ceased to be fashionable elsewhere.

The earliest known reference to the term 'country dance' is in 1579 when it literally meant dances practised by country people. When English country dancing was taken up in France after about 1715 the term was perverted into *contre danse*. In this way the French pinpointed the characteristic of the dances in which a set number of couples often danced face to face in two lines. It was in that sense too that the term was translated into the Italian *contradanza* and the German *Kontre Tanz* and it was as 'contra dances' that the term became known in eastern America much later on. The main point, however, is that whether the implication was informality (as opposed to courtliness) or neighbourliness the term meant much the same wherever or by whomever the dances were practised.

This informality of folk dancing is certainly the feature that appeals today: in many of the dances people link up in a neighbourly, sociable manner either in lines, circles or square sets. This urge to link up and dance in lines can occasionally be seen at public festivities like royal celebrations and even at modern discotheques. English country dancing also had a unique appeal to an urban society as much as to a rural one. It has remained fresh and open to new ideas and influences and thus appeals to modern people, young and old, both in England and abroad. Certainly it is a form of folk dancing in which any newcomer can quickly and readily participate without the rigmarole of learning complicated steps. Folk dancing in England has now come to mean an occasion that appeals to whole families or to individuals, to people of all ages and of all backgrounds, who can enjoy dancing for its own sake, using largely traditional material. The then Princess Elizabeth summed it up very well at her Canadian square

English country dancing. This is a former country dance display team then known as the Sunday Club, dancing in the garden of Cecil Sharp House, London.

dance in 1949 with her perceptive remark, 'This is the ideal social recreation.'

Where and how to find folk dancing

There are very few English villages which still feature the older traditional dances in their local repertoires. Occasionally one will find traditional dances still being performed at a village dance (especially in Northumberland, Yorkshire or Devon) but to all intents and purposes traditional country dancing in the English countryside has died out and, unlike morris and sword dances, the only continuous link with the past is through individuals.   Fortunately, there are many hundreds of folk-dance and folk-song clubs in England which hold dances in local halls to which the public is welcome. The music is nearly always provided by a live band playing traditional tunes or tunes of their own composition in a traditional style. The main difference with the past is the use of electricity for high-quality amplification, lighting and instrumentation.   There is always a caller or MC (master of ceremonies) at these events. It is a notable feature of English dances that this MC will act not merely as an announcer of 'the next dance' but will also run through each dance so that those who are new, or those who have forgotten, may join in without difficulty. The caller will then provide a prompt call to assist the dancers until all appears to be going well.

Sometimes, where these evenings include 'song spots' or 'dance demonstration spots' by a local morris team for example, they are called 'ceilidhs'. This is originally a Gaelic word much used in Ireland and Scotland, where it means something slightly different, but in England it is now widely used to denote an evening of traditional music, songs and dances, the emphasis being on public participation.   Sometimes these evenings are also advertised as a 'folk dance' or a 'barn dance' although one will occasionally see the latter term used to denote something more in the nature of a discotheque than a traditional event. The term 'Country and Western night' can also sometimes be misleading for some seeking an evening of traditional English dancing. Much depends upon the person or persons organising the event. Many members of the public become involved at one time or another in their lives in folk dancing, apart from school activities, in barn dances run by parent teachers' associations, church clubs, drama clubs, sports clubs and so on, or in private events to celebrate a wedding or a birthday or some similar event. The caller will always have a repertoire of dances suitable for the non-initiated. To those involved in the modern revival movement these events are of prime importance because they establish a vital contact with a much wider public in what is a happy and often hilarious occasion.

9
What the old morris dancers said

Volume one, number one, of the *English Folk Dance Society Journal of 1914* included an article by Cecil Sharp based on gleanings from his notebooks in which he jotted down, besides details of the dances, a wealth of useful contemporary general comments on dancing. These sayings throw a lively insight into morris dancing at the end of the nineteenth century. They demonstrate, more vividly than straightforward description can, the pride that many of the surviving dancers had, not only in their dances but also in their feats of youthful athleticism. They also include some useful tips, which are still valid, on teaching as well as performing the dances.

'Never dance flat footed, always on your toe' (Benjamin Moss of Ascott-under-Wychwood, Oxfordshire).

'You must step out forward; you've got to shiver your legs in the capers and that'll fetch the sweat out on you' (an old dancer of North Leigh, Oxfordshire). Speaking of another dancer, he said, 'He was as lissome as a cat; an out-and-out dancer, like on wires.'

Dancers often impressed the need to use light shoes. Harry Taylor of Longborough, Gloucestershire, once said, 'Can't dance in heavy shoes, can't get off the ground. I always used light shoes, well nailed. Must have nails when you dance at Stow as stones so cruel.' Daniel Lock of Minster Lovell, Oxfordshire, also said, 'We couldn't dance in heavy boots with nails but had to use a nice light pair.'

'In jumping, start off with both feet and keep them touching side by side when they come to the ground' (Harry Taylor of Longborough again).

'He was as stiff as a poker, he was: he could make the bells rattle' (Joseph Druce of Ducklington, Oxfordshire).

'He were too squabby about the back to be a dancer; he were lissome according to what he was, but there were plenty of fellows in Field Town who could lick he at dancin'' (Benjamin Moss again).

'They capered as high off the ground as that table, always as high as they could' (Mr Franklin of Field Town or Leafield, Oxfordshire).

'Never dance too young. We began about twenty and then we could stand it; but we couldn't manage it before' (Joseph Druce).

'I was that lissome when I were young, though I look so heavy; and when I danced the last step I could jump on that table' (George Steptoe, Field Town).

'Keep your knees straight; always turn outward; and never let your heels touch the ground – if you did touch with your heels it cost you threepence because it was sure to fetch the tops off some of your bells' (Michael Johnson, Ilmington, Warwickshire).

'We always put the tall 'uns in front, short 'uns behind' (Harry Taylor).

'Put your best men on the near side and the duffers on the other; we never cared so long as we had three good 'uns behind' (Harry Taylor).

There were also some sad remarks as to why many eventually had to stop dancing the morris.

'We didn't dance for money but for sport; we were generally out of pocket over the dancing-mush shure to' (Benjamin Moss of Ascott again).

'We gave up dancing because no one would give anything, so it got like begging which we didn't like' (Benjamin Moss).

'We wern't patternised enough and that was why we stopped, because it didn't take long to dance through a fifteen shilling pair of shoes' (Daniel Lock).

'The morris was given up because people got so proud; so when the men got too old to dance there was no one to take their places' (William Jerdin of Ducklington, Oxfordshire).

Many made the valid point of the important relationship between tune and dance movement.

'If a man doesn't know the tune he can't dance' (Benjamin Moss).

'We used to learn the songs and then there was no trouble; for the steps are just as the words be' (Joseph Druce).

'Our men were always so clean in their dancing; they used to put their steps in so neatly. There was no doubt the fiddler had a lot to do with that' (William Jerdin).

'I can give you some tunes because I was always very quick in the ear; I can give them to you just as they used to be played without any fly notes' (Daniel Lock).

The duration of a dance always varied according to circumstances and was usually determined by the fiddler, who decreed which figures should be repeated or omitted and when the dance should be brought to an end. The dancers were always very particular about the way they finished a dance. One veteran dancer said, 'Always try to make your "stops" well.'

There were also comments on dress.

'We wore white breeches with stockings but some hadn't got legs big enough, so wore trousers' (Benjamin Moss). He also said, 'Girls have got things for their use and men have got things for their use, and the morris is for men.'

William Kimber of Headington Quarry, Oxfordshire, however, always said that women should not be prevented. He said that, after all, they had started the revival and that 'some could whack half the men at dancing a jig..... they dances a damn sight neater than half (the men) do.'

William Kimber also had good advice on teaching. 'Say you wants to point out something very particular, never stand in front of them – that's the wrong way of pointing out how to dance because my left leg's facing your right. Well how do you make them match? A dancer should stand perfectly upright – I don't mean rigid – I mean upright, flexible, but you dances from your hips, your knees and your feet, that's what you dance with. And your hands are to give you balance. And another good tip when you're dancing: learn to keep your mouth shut.'

10
How to get involved

How to learn social folk dancing

Having become involved for the first time, many people often want to find out more, for example, about the dances or the steps and they ask what books they should buy. The answers are that there are indeed printed sources describing all these matters but that the best method is participation and observation of the real thing, to go to as many events as possible and to build up experience. Much of the technique can be learned as one goes along on: listening to the music, phrasing and timing one's movements, reacting with other dancers, poise, when to use free expression or when to be restrained and so on. One can soon learn how to do a right and left hand star, a basket, a ladies' chain, a figure of eight, the various ways to set or balance and swing, a grand chain, a right and left four and so on. There are many sorts of stepping that one can pick up: single step or double step, schottische step, skip-change-step, pas-de-basque step, rant or polka step and waltz step. The main advice is to start moving with the other dancers, listen to the music and fill in the details as one goes along. It helps to remember that, since one only has two feet, the permutations are limited to basically single or double steps, and one should keep one's feet close together and under the body. One should also keep a look-out for workshops on dance technique held either by local clubs or by the numerous festivals and courses around the country.

How to teach the dances

In many ways teaching is also a good way to learn. There is a large number of modern books with dance notations and most MCs these days have their own collections of dances. Probably the best source of dance notations for a well-rounded programme is still to be found in the collection of *Community Dances Manuals* published by the English Folk Dance and Song Society and available from the Folk Shop at Cecil Sharp House in London. For those who wish to advance there are the numerous collections of Playford or eighteenth-century dances which were at one time the main repertoire of the first revival movement. The main point to remember about all these publications is that they should be regarded as *aide-*

mémoires and that in the early days of teaching or learning the first experience of a dance should be doing it, backed up by the written word, for in that way alone can the characteristics of the dance emerge. Many teachers go to public dances, see a dance they like and make a note of the movements there and then. People doing this (incidentally, there should be no copyright problems but it is polite to ask the MC) should note the following:

1. *The shape of the dance*, e.g. longways progressive, longways whole set, circle, Sicilian circle (couple facing couple), double Sicilian (two couples facing two couples), square or couple dance.

2. *The type of music used*, e.g. jig (fast or slow), reel, hornpipe (fast or slow), schottische, waltz, slip jig or other.

3. *The length of each dance figure.* Most of the music comes in eight-bar phrases and most tunes have two parts, an A and a B, for example in the familiar tune 'Cock of the North'. These eight-bar phrases are quite distinctive and act as a signal to the dancers to change to the next movement (the reaction is usually instinctive). For a typical dance there will be two lots of A and two lots of B, making a total of thirty-two bars. Some dances are forty-eight bars long, for which there will be A1, A2, B1, B2, A3, B3, or there may be a tune like 'Sweets of May' which is A1, A2, B1, B2, C1, C2, a three-part tune. The main thing is to note the total number of bars for each figure of a dance. Incidentally, the dancers will usually be totally unaware of all this but *will* notice if the band leaves out an A or a B, such is the way the dances fit the music.

4. *The number of times* a dance is taken through, although this is often optional.

5. *Whether the dance is 'proper' or 'improper'*, in other words whether the first couple is on their own side or have changed over. In some dances, like 'Double change sides' from Devon, or in most of the New England longways dances, the first couple start off on the wrong side and change back when they become a second couple.

Actual teaching or 'calling' techniques are another matter altogether. There are pamphlets to help and workshops are

Musicians with the Winster Morris Dancers, Derbyshire (see also the front cover). Three melodeons tuned in G/D together produce the required crisp strident music so essential these days in noisy streets.

held, or one can again rely on perceptive observation, or all three.

Morris and sword dancing

Most morris or sword-dance teams will welcome new dancers from scratch, operating on the well-established strategy that new blood replaces old. The amount of time required before a new member is allowed to dance out in the team's costume varies from side to side: some insist on a fairly long term of apprenticeship; others push their new members out quite quickly. Much depends on the style, complexity, characteristics and depth of teamwork required. A few sides even insist on a residential qualification: one has to live in the named locality of the side. Whatever the conditions, newcomers should respect the requirements but not be put off by them. The main thing is that there is a much wider choice than there was in the 1970s and one does not have to travel far. Apart from a warm welcome one should look for good teaching, good music, insistence on smart turn-out and good manners with the public. These usually all go together, as does the reverse. The rewards are: a good social ambience, good fun, plenty of physical activity, travel and variety. Many teams get invited abroad to Europe but some have been as far afield as Japan or America. There are also exceptional and not-so-serious occasions: one team danced in the basket of a hot-air balloon over the Oxfordshire countryside; one morris dancer on a round-the-world yacht race danced a jig while rounding Cape Horn; one team danced at 30,000 feet in a jumbo jet. There are also the drawbacks: wet weather, apathetic or hostile audiences, unpleasant publicans, injuries arising out of insufficient warming up or care of limbs and the inevitable tiffs among members.

Practical morris

Many people may be rather nervous about their first visit to a morris or sword side but once the ice is broken there should be few problems. Morris dancing is mostly performed with two rows of dancers facing each other, sometimes three facing three or four facing four (more for north-west or border morris). Basically the dances have two parts. The first is a common figure which in Cotswold morris is much like a country-dance figure, foot-up, back-to-back, rounds; this is performed to the first part of the tune or the A music and is common to all or most of the dances of a certain tradition or village. The second part of the dance is the distinctive figure or chorus and is danced to the second part of the tune or the B music. This part consists of the distinctive stick clashing, hand clapping, handkerchief waving or other characterisation. Somebody once described this as the acting part of the dance because it expresses the main feature. The steps basically consist of either a two-step (one hop, two hop step) or a four-step (one two three hop, step). All dances have distinctive details (arm movements, turns, capers, jumps, etc) and distinctive rhythms and tempi. Some teams dance quite fast, others quite slowly with the emphasis on great leaps and jumps. It is not really possible to learn the dances from a book: 'Any man who endeavours to learn the dances from (the book) without previous knowledge of the morris is likely to gain nothing but a headache' (Introduction to *A Handbook on Morris Dancing* by Lionel Bacon, published by the Morris Ring). In other words the best way to learn is from a team dancing in their own special way. This should not put people off and good advice would be, after a basic run-down on the steps and figures, to join in, to be observant but above all to move with the team and to fill in the multifarious details later with the help of a good teacher.

Most morris sides have three distinctive officers: the *foreman* is the teacher; the *squire* is the captain or chairman of the team and is supposed to take decisions; and the *bagman* is the secretary and treasurer who writes the letters and looks after the 'bag' or collection and other finances.

Morris music

The origin of tunes used for morris dancing makes a fascinating study. A large number of them are derived from popular songs and tunes of the eighteenth century, with others from the nineteenth century. There are many other sources. The familiar tune 'Greensleeves', dating from the time of Henry VIII, re-emerges in a different rhythm as the 'Bacca Pipes' jig. 'Princess Royal' is derived from a tune published by Walsh in 1730 and used for the song 'Arethusa' but that may be derived from a tune written by the blind Irish harpist O'Carolan at the end of the seventeenth century. 'Shepherds Hey' could be older still. The Headington Quarry morris men have a processional dance which uses 'La Mourisque' from *The Danserye* published by the Flemish composer Susato in 1551. Moreover they were using this tune long before the revival of interest in Renaissance music. 'I'll go and enlist for a Sailor' is a nineteenth-century music-hall song tune. *The Beggars' Opera,* written by John Gay in 1727, is full of tunes familiar to morris dancers, for example the last number 'Lumps of Plum Pudding', but then the music for that opera was a compilation of popular songs of the day. Some tunes used are from the twentieth century. The instruments used are those which carry most volume outdoors without the assistance of amplification, like button accordions or melodeons, concertinas, piano accordions, three-hole pipes and tabors and, for processional morris, brass instruments and drums. Violins and other stringed instruments are used to a lesser extent these days.

Sword dancing

Here the technique is very different from morris dancing. There are two sorts of sword dancing, long sword and rapper. Strictly speaking, the swords are not swords but strips of metal, either rigid or flexible, with handles. Their main purpose is to link the dancers together during the performance of the distinctive figures. Because of this linking, the demands on teamwork are much more intense than in morris dancing. The steps are a lilting walking step for long sword and a fast tap stepping for rapper. Initially both sorts of stepping are not difficult but they require much practice subsequently to fit in with the characteristics of a particular team. Some teams perform only sword dances but a large number of morris-dance teams include sword dancing in their repertoire. Both sorts of sword dancing require good basic skills, good presentation and a good sense of native tradition.

Great Western Morris from Exeter dancing a Cotswold stick dance at Towersey Village Festival, Oxfordshire, August 1993.

11
Useful events, workshops and addresses

For a full list of local dance clubs people can apply to any of the organisations listed at the end of this chapter. Local libraries and tourist information offices may also have lists. Some clubs advertise for new members in the local press.

There are also important folk festivals lasting a week or a weekend which organise among other things a wide choice of dance workshops. The largest folk festival is held at **Sidmouth** in Devon (known as the Sidmouth International Festival of Folk Arts). This event, lasting over a week, consists of displays by British and foreign teams as well as a large number of events in which members of the public may join, including a comprehensive choice of dance, song and music workshops. It is held at the end of July and into the beginning of August or during the first complete week in August. A similar event lasting a week but run on smaller lines takes place in the second week of August at **Broadstairs** in Kent (known as the Broadstairs Folk Week). The last complete week in August sees the Whitby Folk Week held at **Whitby**, North Yorkshire. There is also the famous International Eisteddfod at **Llangollen**, Clwyd, held every year in July. Strictly speaking this is a Welsh event but English dance teams do frequently appear and compete. There are many other folk festivals held during weekends throughout the year, organised by local song or dance clubs or by groups of hard-working individuals. A publication listing them, *Folk Festival Guide*, is available from the Folk Shop at Cecil Sharp House (see below).

Finally, there is in London the well-known folk music centre known as Cecil Sharp House. It is the headquarters of the English Folk Dance and Song Society and was named after the society's founder, Cecil Sharp. It contains dance halls, the Vaughan Williams Memorial Library of books, records and tapes, the Folk Shop (instruments, books, records, tapes, compact discs, souvenirs, etc), a canteen and a bar. It is in Regent's Park Road, north-east of Regent's Park, and the nearest underground railway station is Camden Town. Many song and dance events, concerts and training sessions are organised here. Parallel to this is a residential folk-music centre known as Halsway Manor, owned by the Halsway

Manor Society, at Crowcombe near Taunton in Somerset. It also has a library and organises song, dance and musical courses and events during the year.

There are many organisations, most of them voluntary, connected with most aspects of folk dancing and here is a list of them.

The English Folk Dance and Song Society (EFDSS), Cecil Sharp House, 2 Regent's Park Road, London NW1 7AY. Telephone: 071-485 2206. The main aims and objectives of this society are discussed in the text but they can be summarised generally as being to maintain and encourage the best in England's own folk music, song and dance. It has an Education Department supported by the Sports Council and publishes a *Folk Music Journal* once a year and a quarterly magazine, *English Dance and Song*. It also publishes an annual *Folk Directory* and can supply comprehensive lists of festivals, major events, dates of customary events and lists of local clubs. The headquarters building also contains the invaluable Folk Shop.

The Vaughan Williams Memorial Library is situated at the above address and is the major source of information on the work of the collectors of England's heritage of folk music, song and dance and traditional custom. Its collection of material is unique in England.

Halsway Manor Society Limited is a residential folk centre set on the southern slopes of the Quantock Hills in west Somerset. Its range of activities is described in the text. The address is Halsway Manor, Crowcombe, Taunton, Somerset TA4 4BD. Telephone: 09848 274.

Folk Camps Society Limited organises activity holidays for all ages, either catering or self-catering, both in England and in France, during the major holiday season. Many people in the past have had their first experience of folk music, song and dance at the informal sessions held at these camps. Write to the Secretary, Folk Camps Society Ltd, 27 Peter Street, Taunton, Somerset TA2 4BY.

The Morris Ring was founded in 1934 by six clubs of morris men to organise meetings and to help teams exchange information. The Ring now consists of 186 full member sides of morris and sword dance teams plus 86 associate sides. All the member sides have to be all-male and have to pass an entry test showing that their dancing and music are of good quality, that they are viable in numbers, have a stable immediate past and a viable future and that they are sociable. The aims of the Ring today are 'to encourage the performance of the morris and to maintain its traditions and to bring into contact all men's morris clubs or teams'. The Ring organises the big meeting of morris dancers at Thaxted, Essex, at the end of May and usually six other big Ring meetings hosted by local clubs throughout the year. The address of their Bagman or secretary is 13 Belper Road, Kilburn, Belper, Derbyshire DE56 0LP. (Please send a stamped and addressed envelope if writing.)

The Morris Federation was originally founded in 1975 by Betty Reynolds to help the growing number of women's teams being formed at that time and was originally known as the 'Women's Morris Federation'. 1980 saw the acceptance of mixed and joint teams as members and in 1982 membership was opened to any team, regardless of gender. Accordingly the word 'Women's ' was dropped from the name and the Morris Federation came into being in 1983. Since then the membership has grown to about 300 teams. The aims of the Federation are to encourage and maintain interest in the practice of morris dancing by women and men of all ages; to provide a channel of communication between member sides and to encourage the improvement of standards of dancing among its members. The address of the secretary is 36 Foxbury Road, Bromley, Kent BR1 4DQ. That of the President is 69 Mickleton Road, Earlsdon, Coventry CV5 6PP. (Please enclose a stamped and addressed envelope if writing.)

The Hobby Horse Club of England is an organisation for children under thirteen and runs workshops in clog, morris, sword, social dance and song, customs and teaching and leadership. It runs festival activities and days of dance and consists of about 27 separate clubs in England. The current secretary lives at 16 Heathgate, Hertford Heath, Hertford SG13 7PH. (Please enclose a stamped and addressed envelope if writing.)

Some of the addresses of the voluntary organisations may change in the course of time. If this is the case the new address can usually be obtained from the EFDSS at Cecil Sharp House in London.

12
Calendar of folk-dance events

The following list is for the most part arranged by months. In most cases it is impossible to give the exact date of an event since this often varies from year to year. However, if the reader looks up the details of the event in the appropriate section of this book (that is the ritual ceremonial or the social dance) he will usually be able to work out the date. If this is not possible, or if there is any doubt, the reader should contact one of the organisations listed in chapter 11. There are many other shows and festivals organised from year to year but not mentioned here, which they can tell you about. Ask for the *Folk Festival Guide* published annually.

January
Whittlesey, Cambridgeshire: Straw Bear Festival

Easter Saturday
Bacup, Lancashire: Britannia Coconut Dancers

May
Padstow, Cornwall: 'Obby Oss' celebrations
Minehead, Somerset: Hobby Horse celebrations
Helston, Cornwall: Furry Dance
Chippenham, Wiltshire: Folk Festival
Eastbourne, East Sussex: Folk Festival
Great Wishford, Wiltshire: Oak Apple Day
Thaxted, Essex: Morris dancing
Combe Martin, Devon: Hunting of the Earl of Rone
Rochester, Kent: Chimney Sweeps' May Festival

Spring Bank Holiday Monday
Bampton and Headington, Oxfordshire: morris dancing

June
Abingdon, Oxfordshire, morris dancing
Salisbury, Wiltshire: Hob-nob

July
Redcar, Cleveland: Folk Festival

August
Sidmouth, Devon: International Festival of Folk Arts
Whitby, North Yorkshire: folk week
Saddleworth, Lancashire: rushbearing
South Zeal, Okehampton, Devon: Dartmoor Folk Festival
Billingham, Cleveland: International Folklore Festival
Broadstairs, Kent: folk week
Towersey, Oxfordshire: village festival

September
Abbots Bromley, Staffordshire: Horn Dance
Bromyard, Hereford and Worcester: folk festival

Boxing Day
Handsworth and Grenoside, South Yorkshire: sword dancing
Flamborough, Humberside: sword dancing
Greatham, Cleveland: sword dancing and mummers' play

Sticks and Steps, a junior team (average age ten) from Cheshire, dancing north-west clog morris at the Towersey Village Festival in Oxfordshire, August 1993.

13
Further reading

Bacon, L. *A Handbook of Morris Dances*. The Morris Ring, 1974.

Barrand, A.G. *Six Fools and a Dancer: The Timeless Way of The Morris* (with notations and dance instructions). Northern Harmony, Plainfield, Vermont, USA, 1991.

Buckland, T. (editor). 'Proceedings of the Traditional Dance Conference held at Crewe and Alsager College of Higher Education, Alsager', *Traditional Dance*, 1-6. Crewe and Alsager College of Higher Education, 1982-8.

Buckland, T. (editor). 'Definitions of Folk Dance: Some Explorations', *Folk Music Journal,* 4, no. 4, 315-32, 1983.

Buckland, T. (editor). 'Institutions and Ideology in the Dissemination of Morris Dances in the Northwest of England', *1991 Yearbook for Traditional Music*, 23, pages 53-67.

Burton, A. *Rush Bearing*. Brook & Chrystal, Manchester, 1891.

Cawte, E.C. *An Index to Cecil J Sharp: The Morris Book, 5 volumes, 1911-1924* . The Morris Ring and The Centre for English Cultural Tradition and Language, University of Sheffield,1983.

Cawte, E.C., Helm, A., Marriot, R.J., and Peacock, N. 'A Geographical Index of the Ceremonial Dance in Great Britain', *Journal of the English Folk Dance and Song Society*, 9, no. 1, pages 1-41, 1960.

Cawte, E.C., Helm, A., Marriot, R.J. and Peacock, N. 'Addenda and Corrigenda', *Journal of the English Folk Dance and Song Society*, 9, no. 2, pages 93-5, 1961.

Chandler, K. *Ribbons, Bells and Squeaking Fiddles: The Social History of Morris Dancing in the English South Midlands, 1660-1900.* The Folklore Society, Tradition I, Tradition II, and Hisarlik Press, Enfield Lock, Middlesex, 1993.

Chandler, K. *Morris Dancing in the English South Midlands 1660-1900 : A Chronological Gazetteer.* The Folklore Society, Tradition I, Tradition II, and Hisarlik Press, Enfield Lock, Middlesex, 1993.

Corrsin, S.D. *Sword Dancing in Central and Northern Europe: An Annotated Bibliography.* Country Dance and Song Society of America, 1990.

English Folk Dance and Song Society. *The Community Dances Manuals.* Volumes 1-7. English Folk Dance and Song

Society, 1947-67.

Frazer, J.G. *The Golden Bough, A Study in Comparative Religion* (1907-15). Third edition, 12 volumes. Macmillan, paperback 1957, reprinted 1976.

Hardy, T. *Under the Greenwood Tree or The Mellstock Quire. A Rural Painting of the Dutch School* (1872). Macmillan, 1974. See especially pages 52-9.

Heaney, M. *An Introductory Bibliography on Morris Dancing.* Vaughan Williams Memorial Library Leaflet no. 19, addenda. English Folk Dance and Song Society, 1985, 1990.

Heaney, M., and Forrest, J. *Annals of Early Morris.* Centre for English Cultural Tradition and Language, University of Sheffield, in association with The Morris Ring, 1991.

Hall, Reg. *Scan Tester, Sussex Musician 1887-1972. 'I Never Played Too Many Posh Dances'.* Musical Traditions, Rochford, 1990.

Jones, D. *The Roots of Welsh Border Morris: The Welsh Border Morris Dances of Herefordshire, Worcestershire and Shropshire.* Putley, Ledbury, 1988.

Judge, R. 'Mary Neal and The Esperance Morris', *Folk Music Journal*, 5, no. 5, pages 545-91, 1989.

Judge, R. 'D'Arcy Ferris and The Bidford Morris', *Folk Music Journal*, 4, no. 5, pages 443-80, 1989.

Malcolmson, R.W. *Popular Recreations in English Society 1700-1850.* Cambridge University Press, 1973.

Metherell, C. *An Introductory Bibliography on Clog and Step Dance.* Vaughan Williams Memorial Library leaflet no. 22. English Folk Dance and Song Society, London, 1993.

Morris Dancing in the South Midlands. Chandler Publications, Eynsham, 1983-7.

The Morris Ring and The Morris Federation. *The Evolving Morris. Proceedings of a One-Day Conference, Cecil Sharp House, London, 1992.* The Morris Ring, The Morris Federation and Open Morris, 1992.

Needham, J. 'The Geographical Distribution of the English Ceremonial Dance Traditions', *Journal of the English Folk Dance and Song Society*, 3, no. 1, pages 1-45, 1936.

Sharp, C.J. *The Morris Book.* 5 parts. Novello, London, 1907-14.
    Part 1 with H.C. MacIlwaine; first edition 1907; second edition 1919; reprinted, EP Publishing, Wakefield, 1974.
    Part 2 with H.C. MacIlwaine; first edition 1909; second edition 1919; reprinted, EP Publishing, Wakefield, 1974.
    Part 3 with H.C. MacIlwaine; first edition 1910; second edition 1924; reprinted, EP Publishing, Wakefield, 1974.

Part 4; first edition 1911; reprinted, EP Publishing, Wakefield 1975.

Part 5 with G. Butterworth; first edition 1913; reprinted, EP Publishing, Wakefield, 1975.

Sharp, C. J. *The Country Dance Books*. 6 parts. 1909-22.

Part 1; first edition 1909; second edition, revised and edited by M. Karpeles, 1934; reprinted, EP Publishing, Wakefield, 1972.

Part 2; first edition 1911; second edition 1913; third edition 1927; reprinted, EP Publishing, Wakefield, 1972.

Part 3 with G. Butterworth; first edition 1912; second edition 1927; reprinted, EP Publishing, Wakefield, 1975.

Part 4 with G. Butterworth; first edition 1916; second edition 1918; third edition 1927; reprinted, EP Publishing, Wakefield, 1975.

Part 5 with M. Karpeles; first edition 1918; reprinted, EP Publishing, Wakefield, 1975.

Part 6; first edition 1922; second edition 1927; reprinted, EP Publishing, Wakefield, 1976.

Sharp, C. J. *The Sword Dances of Northern England*. 3 parts. 1911-13.

Part 1; first edition 1911; second edition, edited by M. Karpeles, 1950; reprinted, EP Publishing, Wakefield, 1977.

Part 2; first edition 1913; second edition, edited by M. Karpeles, 1951; reprinted, EP Publishing, Wakefield, 1977.

Part 3; first edition 1913; second edition, edited by M. Karples, 1951; reprinted, EP Publishing, Wakefield, 1977.

Stone, T. *Rattle Up My Boys*. An occasional broadsheet for those with an interest in longsword dance. 6 Priory Road, Sale, Cheshire M33 2BR.

Sughrue, C.M. 'Proceedings of the Contemporary Morris and Sword Dancing Conference, University of Sheffield, 1988', *Lore and Language*, 6, no. 2.

Sughrue, C.M. 'Some Thoughts on the Tradition versus Revival Debate', *Traditional Dance*, 5/6, pages 184-90, 1988.

Underdown, David. *Revel, Riot and Rebellion. Popular Politics and Culture in England 1603-1660*. Oxford University Press, 1985.

Index

Page numbers in italic refer to illustrations.